CAP IN HAND

CAP IN HAND

How Salary Caps are Killing Pro Sports
and Why the Free Market
Could Save Them

BRUCE DOWBIGGIN
with RYAN GAUTHIER

Published by ECW Press
665 Gerrard Street East
Toronto, Ontario, Canada M4M 1Y2
416-694-3348 / info@ecwpress.com

Editor for the Press: Michael Holmes
Cover design: David A. Gee

LIBRARY AND ARCHIVES CANADA
CATALOGUING IN PUBLICATION

Dowbiggin, Bruce, author

Cap in hand : how salary caps are killing pro
sports and why the free market could save them /
Bruce Dowbiggin with Ryan Gauthier.

Issued in print and electronic formats.
ISBN 978-1-77041-393-1 (hardcover)
ISBN 978-1-77305-238-0 (HTML)
ISBN 978-1-77305-239-7 (PDF)

1. Professional sports—Economic aspects—
Canada. 2. Professional sports—Economic
aspects—United States. I. Gauthier, Ryan,
author II. Title.

GV716.D69 2018   338.4'77960971   C2018-902539-5

C2018-902540-9

The publication of *Cap in Hand* has been generously supported by the Government of Canada
through the Canada Book Fund. *Ce livre est financé en partie par le gouvernement du Canada.* We also
acknowledge the contribution of the Government of Ontario through the Ontario Book Publishing
Tax Credit and the Ontario Media Development Corporation.

Ontario
Ontario Media Development
Corporation

Canada

PRINTED AND BOUND IN CANADA   PRINTING: FRIESENS   5   4   3   2   1

MIX
Paper from
responsible sources
FSC® C016245

PREFACE VII
INTRODUCTION 1

PART 1
THE CONTRACTS THAT SHAPED
PROFESSIONAL SPORT 13

—

1.1 Babe Ruth 13
1.2 Curt Flood 25
1.3 Catfish Hunter 45
1.4 Bobby Hull 55
1.5 Magic and Bird 63
1.6 Reggie White 70
1.7 Wayne Gretzky 78
1.8 Shaquille O'Neal 86
1.9 Alex Rodriguez 95
1.10 David Beckham 103
1.11 LeBron James 110

—

PART 2
SPORTS AND THE LAW:
THE FINE PRINT 119

—

2.1 How Antitrust/Competition Law
Works in Sports 121
2.2 If the Shoe Fits:
Labor Law Applied to Sports 126
2.3 The Entry Draft 133
2.4 Free Agency Ain't Free 138
2.5 So What the Heck Is a Salary Cap, Then? 146

2.6 Exceptions to the Cap 150
2.7 Cap Circumvention 153
2.8 Collusion 160
2.9 The Role of the Commissioner
in All of This 163
2.10 If the Cap Don't Fit . . . 165

—

PART 3 ·
BRINGING BACK REAL COMPETITION 171

—

3.1 Rewarding Success, Not Failure 175
3.2 It's My Parity and I'll Cry If I Want To 180
3.3 A System You Can Bet On 187
3.4 Leveling the Playing Field by
Restricting Free Agency 192
3.5 There's a Draft in Here:
The Amateur Draft Doesn't Level Competition 198
3.6 Attempts to Rebalance the Draft 204
3.7 Moving Beyond the Draft 208
3.8 Too Beat to Compete:
How Salary Caps Dumb Down Play 210
3.9 Innovate or Die: Unless You Have a Cap 213
3.10 Then There's Soccer: The Benefits
to a Non-Salary-Capped League 215
3.11 Does Parity Pay? 221
3.12 What About Soccer's Corruption? 224
3.13 Okay, Smart Guys,
What Would Work Better? 226

—

PREFACE

In 1987, baseball's Boswell, Bill James, was frustrated with Major League Baseball's labor stoppages and the decline of the minor leagues. Bill is frustrated a lot of the time. The inability to accept "given wisdom" produces much of his best work on sports (and crime, too). So he wrote an essay entitled "Revolution." In this case, he thought the minor leagues as they existed (and still exist) "were an abomination in the sight of the Lord . . . if you're selling a sport and the players don't care about winning that's not a sport. That's a fraud. Minor league baseball today is exactly what the 1919 World Series was: a charade, a rip-off, an exhibition masquerading as a contest."

He described how Hall of Fame manager Earl Weaver used to distort the box scores he sent to the Baltimore Orioles because he was playing a prospect at first base. The Orioles wanted the prospect to play third base. So Weaver fibbed in the paperwork. As Bill writes, "Earl wanted to win" but, to do so, had to resort to subterfuge. "That's a disgraceful situation." Bill was no less disgusted with how leagues were shutting down their business every couple of years to argue about why the free market was not the best way to determine the value of a player's compensation.

In his ire, Bill went looking for a better model that would allow folks in non-major-league cities to have a team that tried to win. Enter "Revolution."

Bill proposed that, as opposed to limiting the number of teams in MLB to protect parity, the market was perfectly capable of sustaining many more teams than it does now. He thought it could run into the hundreds. Maybe as many as 240. (There was a lot of math involved the argument, but suffice to say, it involved the U.S. population being 240 million at the time.) All it might take was letting the free market sort out the level at which those cities might best compete.

In "Revolution," he pointed out that a free market in sports teams and athletes existed at one time and could work as well again if the monopolists of MLB and the NFL, NBA and NHL would simply relent from their salary-restraint schemes and reserve-clause models. The piece is classic Bill: "At first there was no reserve clause. This was a sort of primordial soup for baseball, and the players would just drift from team to team as suited themselves." He then described how today's model of limited movement and mediocrity evolved as big cities subordinated smaller cities using a farm system that prioritized development over winning. Until the point where today — with the cooperation of player unions — elite talent is spread as thinly as possible at the major-league level, movement of players is grossly distorted and mediocrity is rewarded via amateur drafts and equalization payments.

None of this has to be, he pointed out, if teams could operate in their own interests, not the interests of the league. If a free market worked, you would have teams play at the level they could afford, players sold up the developmental food chain for profit and a dynamic incentive to improve. No salary caps, amateur drafts, Rule 5 drafts, recallable waivers or back-diving contracts. Just the noise of the free market.

Bill knew that Nellies like me would complain that this might not be very stable.

Competition isn't always pretty. Teams would fold, go bankrupt sometimes, use near-naked usherettes in a cheap attempt to boost attendance, pull out in the middle of the night without paying their debts — all the things businesses do . . . Baseball would be less stable. It would change more rapidly than it ever has, in part because each league would be learning from the experiences of the other leagues. But it would be changing because it was growing, and it would be growing toward a baseball world that is larger, stronger, richer, more diverse and more fair to the fans. It can happen.

All it would take is for the U.S. Justice Department to revoke baseball's antitrust exemption (more on this in the next sections). Order MLB to divest itself of its farm systems. And tell the player unions that they shouldn't be subverting competition and labor law in collective bargaining. Let the baseball people go.

When I read "Revolution," it was a transformative moment in how I looked at sports leagues. I had bought all the propaganda they put out about winning, stability, parity and how the restrictive systems they used were the only path to create a better sport. (Which was significant because I was working as a sports journalist at CBC at the time.) Even when they shut down their sports to create an even more pernicious system to crush market value, I saw it as the cost of doing business. Until Bill deconstructed my accepted notion of the sports industry, I had simply assumed this was the way it must be. To be competitive, the system had to be regulated to death. As I say, bullshit. From that day on, I've never looked at organized pro sports in the same fashion. That was also probably the day I started the move from being a liberal to a conservative.

(Ironically, when I asked Bill about the article in 2017, he couldn't remember having written it. His online followers found it in a book called *This Time Let's Not Eat the Bones*. Here, I'd been massively influenced by his insights into the dynamics of sports leagues, yet Bill couldn't remember it. But when you have as much original thought flowing through your brain as Bill does, I suspect this happens occasionally.)

So yes, "Revolution" underpins this book. Like Bill, I look at the product sold to fans and see a pale copy of what it might be if the market could guide the best players to the best teams, whose ingenuity and innovation (hello, Bill Belichick) would then inspire everyone to do better and present a better show. As we'll see, soccer (outside North America) comes closer to this model than anyone, and it's taking over the world. That is, in part, because soccer has accepted that professional sports have moved beyond the restrictive covenants of the franchise model to a pursuit of an excellent TV/digital product for global consumption.

So here we go. In this book, I'm joined by Ryan Gauthier, a sports law expert who has written extensively on the issues in this book. Please welcome him to the fraternity of those looking to improve pro sports. Remember, anyone who thinks parity is a thing should be made to watch the NHL All-Star Game on a tape loop.

Bruce Dowbiggin, 2017

INTRODUCTION

Russell Wilson might be the most recognizable and successful player in the NFL. The quarterback of the Seattle Seahawks has led them to a Super Bowl win and regular playoff appearances in his first five seasons in the Seahawks uniform. Because of his commercials, Wilson is instantly recognizable to tens of millions of football fans. His dating life is the stuff of non-sports curiosity, too. His divorce and subsequent relationship with singer Ciara have engaged people who might not know a thing about sports.

Wilson is the ideal package for the media-savvy NFL.

And the league is doing everything it can to turn him and his Seahawks into losers.

Jonathan Toews is the star captain of the Chicago Blackhawks. A three-time Stanley Cup champion, he embodies all the virtues that the NHL loves in a player. Hard work, success and charitable ventures off the ice — Toews couldn't be more perfect for a league always short on star power. He's bilingual, too, speaking English and French flawlessly.

The NHL should want one hundred Toewses in the league. But it does everything it can to make sure that he doesn't win another Stanley Cup.

Steph Curry, the star of the Golden State Warriors, is the face of the modern NBA. He's revolutionized the game with his outside shooting, defying the traditional notion of the NBA as a big man's league where titles are supposedly won under the hoop. Boyish, but with a killer's eye in big games, he's taken the Warriors to the NBA Finals multiple times, winning in 2015. He holds the record for most three-point shots made, breaking Ray Allen's record of 269 with 272 in 2012–13, 286 in 2014–15 and a mind-boggling 402 in the 2014–15 season. Off the court, he's in demand for commercials, charitable events and promotions across the globe.

Steph Curry is the NBA's vision made real. The transcendent son of a former player and coach, he has turned a generation of young people on to the league. But the NBA is putting every impediment it can in front of him as he tries to author a legendary career.

Why are pro sports leagues in North America — leagues that live or die with their promotional savvy and communications genius — doing this to their most marketable stars? Moreover, how are they stunting the legacies of players known internationally for their star power?

"I don't know of any space other than the world of sports where there's this notion that we will artificially deflate what someone's able to make, just because," said NBPA director Michele Roberts talking about a collectively bargained policy that has constrained team spending in the NBA since 1984–85. "It's incredibly un-American. My DNA is offended by it."

The answer is called parity. These leagues are propping up a business model from a generation ago with a system of parity that holds that every town with an owner rich enough deserves a team. And that every owner also deserves a fair shot at holding the Vince Lombardi Trophy or Stanley Cup or Larry O'Brien Trophy.

That's a complicated task in a world where, as Boston GM Harry Sinden once told me, there are 30 teams and just one Stanley Cup. Keeping team owners, players, fans, broadcasters, sponsors and others happy is a tricky business. Because just a few markets are large enough, or just a few owners are wealthy enough, to do whatever it takes to assemble the best team, the rampant capitalists of pro sports felt they needed to create a drag on the worth of their star employees. A handicapping system. A way to make sure every dog could have his day.

The latest, and supposedly greatest, leveler is called the salary cap. And it's the most regressive thing that could have happened to the product in the NFL, NHL or NBA. Or to Russell Wilson, Jonathan Toews and Steph Curry. In the service of parity, salary caps dismantle successful teams, reward inept management and rob the fan of the chance to see the very best play the very best without armies of mediocre players and stultifying coaching strategies.

Put simply, the salary cap uses a Soviet-style scythe to level competition in the service of parity. Owners and players decide on a figure for league revenues and then cap salaries by placing a limit on spending by the teams. Each league's salary cap has nuances and differences that only a lawyer could love. In the case of the NHL, teams are given a maximum amount they can spend and a minimum amount that they must spend — a "salary floor." The NBA gives teams previously employing a player a "hometown advantage" to re-sign that player and maintain continuity. The NFL has provisions for a "franchise tag" that allows a club to keep a player for one more year if they pay him the average of the top five players in the league at his position.

You may have noticed that we haven't mentioned Major League Baseball yet. America's pastime, that bastion of "tradition" and "unwritten rules," is more progressive than its competitors, if only marginally. It doesn't use the salary cap. Despite the strenuous efforts of MLB owners through eight labor stoppages dating back to the 1970s, baseball has settled for something called a luxury tax. This system sets a top end for team salaries but also allows clubs to go over that figure if they pay a tax on the overspend. The NBA has managed to create a byzantine system that has both a salary cap and a luxury tax, but it really operates more like the capped leagues.

The salary cap was touted as the best way to allow for even competition among small and large markets. But in the leagues that have harnessed themselves to the salary cap, the percentage of small- and medium-market teams that win is similar to the MLB's. So there appear to be more ways than salary-cap parity to get desired results.

The impetus for salary caps was the franchise model that leagues embraced back in the 1960s. Before that time, leagues would be comprised of teams in no more than a dozen cities. Fans accepted that teams in big markets had advantages. But mostly they recognized that the best managers and the best players should win most of the time. The business model for pro sports ownership before the '60s was an eclectic mix of sponsorship by regional beer companies, cars and men's products (like razor blades), combined with whatever tickets could be sold at the gate. National revenues were almost nonexistent.

But the media and communications revolution of the '60s presented fertile new ground for sports owners looking to expand their profits. Thanks to the ability of new jetliners to carry people from coast to coast in five or six hours, new horizons presented themselves. If the established teams — largely huddled in the northeast corner of the USA — could build toward a continent-wide presence of regional markets, they might just get TV and radio networks to pay impressive figures to broadcast the games nationally, not just regionally. Where once it was only the World Series that commanded a national audience, now leagues could attract advertisers to a regular "game of the week," shown nationally, which could come from three time zones away.

Major League Baseball began the experiment, pushing the New York–based Dodgers and Giants to California, establishing a truly national footprint with franchises in Los Angeles and San Francisco. The NFL, too, went west to establish a beach head on the Pacific coast. As the leagues hoped, the TV money came rolling in. Soon, the NBA and the NHL — eager for the TV money — made it to the west coast, too. By the 1970s, there were fans in over 20 more cities rooting for a local team.

Better than the flood of TV money to established owners was the lure of hefty expansion franchise fees from millionaires anxious to have their own teams in the big leagues. The dream was sports as IKEA, spreading the brand of football, basketball, baseball or hockey to eager consumers as if it were cheap Swedish furniture. Look at the result: An NHL expansion team went for $2 million in 1967; it cost $500 million for the new Las Vegas owners in 2016. (All dollar amounts in this book are in U.S. dollars unless otherwise specified.) There have been no new NFL teams since expansion to Houston in 2002, but there have been relocations. Even the fees for relocations are astronomical, with the NFL's Rams and Chargers paying $600 million each to move to Los Angeles in 2016 and 2017 respectively and the Raiders paying $350 million to move from Oakland to Las Vegas. Values for teams can range from $935 million for the Buffalo Bills to $3.2 billion for the Dallas Cowboys. The NBA's L.A. Clippers sold for $2 billion in 2014.

The only problem with expanding to as many as 30 or 32 teams is the inequity it creates between markets. How could Kansas City or Winnipeg compete evenly with New York City or Los Angeles for players? Who wants to lose all the time or play in a smaller market? In a free market, the established wisdom was that all the best players would gravitate to a few prestigious teams.

In the early years of sport — until the 1950s and '60s for all professional leagues except baseball — teams were allowed to restrain on players through the reserve clause, a system initially supported by the US Supreme Court. In particular, MLB was granted an exemption from American antitrust laws in the 1920s by that court — a situation that persists to this day. With the approval of the judges in several landmark cases brought by athletes, the leagues were able to skirt laws on restraint of trade and monopoly status. Using the baseball example, sports with antitrust exemptions were allowed to define player contracts as open-ended documents, tying players to a team in perpetuity, killing their market value. Although Babe Ruth was able to command a salary driven by his value in the 1920s, few athletes enjoyed the same leverage for the next half century. Any competition for players was quickly stomped out by the leagues.

The 1950s and '60s brought a new generation of athletes and their agents (another innovation). They saw the leagues' increasing profitability and were determined to get a piece of the action that reflected their importance to the product. They sought to shame the courts into enforcing the laws. The players in the NFL, NHL and NBA were successful. Oddly, the most famous of these pioneers were the ones that were unsuccessful before the courts: MLB Players Association director Marvin Miller and star outfielder Curt Flood, who challenged baseball's reserve clause in the courts in 1969, losing before the U.S.

Supreme Court in 1972 — an event that we'll cover later in the book.

Though unsuccessful in overturning MLB's antitrust exemption at the time, Flood's case was a signal for impending free agency in all the major team sports as leagues were engaging in collective bargaining with player unions. Within a decade, the expression "market value" was firmly implanted in the lexicon of the sports business.

Owners did not submit meekly as the first free agents were granted the right to negotiate freely. Faced with having to pay market value for players, the leagues first engaged in scare campaigns, telling the public that free agency was the end of competition as they knew it. If a star player could leave for another team after having completed his obligations under his contract, all the best players would gravitate to the biggest financial centers. The owners' propaganda worked for a time. Fans and players both agreed that maybe this free-agent stuff was dangerous to the sport as they knew it.

But starting with Catfish Hunter's free agency in 1975 (see part 2), the public saw free agency and liked the freedom of players to move to their favorite team. Players, at first reluctant to disbelieve what they'd always been told by owners, soon realized that someone had just opened a bank vault to them. In one sport after the other — hockey finally succumbing in the early '90s after years of collusion with its union — free agency conquered the market. Stars became rich and owners became nervous about controlling the salary spiral.

In their desire to win as quickly as possible, owners were their own worst enemies, creating scarcity where none had existed before. Faced with a shot at a championship, they proved incapable of disciplining themselves when a premium player appeared on the open market, spending more than they ever had before. What was to become of competitive balance if the smaller markets lost all their players to large markets? With the courts suddenly of no help in interpreting contracts their way, owners would need something new to control the insatiable need for one more big contract to guarantee a title or even just a playoff spot.

Enter the salary cap. It allowed leagues the simulacrum of a free market while punishing the marketability of the Russell Wilsons, Jonathan Toewses and Steph Currys. As we'll see, leagues only achieved the salary cap as part of bitter collective bargaining. Players accepted caps in exchange for freedom within the system — along with other perks such as independent arbitration in salary and disciplinary matters.

In their haste to get control of payrolls, owners didn't much concern themselves with how a socialist-style system would affect the quality of play. In a bid to save themselves from each other, they left the details to coaches and general managers who were eager to save their own jobs first. Owners also didn't pay attention to what would happen when the franchise model gave way to a new master: global communications. The sports economy has been changed by the communications revolution that carries games and players' images around the globe. No longer does a league need a team in every town to spread its product.

Cap in Hand is about how the law of unintended consequences diluted talent and dispersed skilled players over too many teams. Sports executives also didn't forsee that under a salary-cap system tied to universal drafts teams might actually deliberately lose — "tank" — for four or five seasons to corner the best talent. The recent example of how the Houston Astros went from worst to first — laughingstock to World Series champ — is sure to be emulated by other franchises who will subject their fans to a lousy product in the hope that they can replicate the success of the Astros.

Leagues are now dominated by coaches obsessed with video and game planning, not inspiration and creativity, who coach not to lose instead of to win. In the words of former Detroit Red Wings star Pavel Datsyuk, "There are not many creative players now . . . It's less and less every year. There's lots of talent, but teams are playing more systems . . . Hockey is so different now." The same can easily be said for all the team sports except basketball, where the small rosters still allow for teams to concentrate stars on a team. No wonder the Golden State Warriors and the NBA have captured a worldwide audience.

Cap in Hand also proposes a way out of this mess. Soccer has demonstrated that the sports world has morphed from the overstocked inventories of the franchise model to one based on matchups of elite teams populated by elite players. Without a salary cap, the beautiful game has allowed for the growth of superteams in smaller leagues. There is no parity in soccer, just the unending quest for the best product possible. As a result, the sport has finally made a breakthrough in North America with a new generation of fans intrigued by the great Lionel Messi, Cristiano Ronaldo, Paul Pogba and Harry Kane.

The story of the salary cap is one played out over generations of contracts and labor decisions. Perhaps the best way to understand the owners' mania at suppressing market value in sports (as opposed to entertainment) is to follow the money. And the money started with Babe Ruth.

PART 1

THE CONTRACTS THAT SHAPED PROFESSIONAL SPORT

1.1 BABE RUTH

"I had a better year than him."

Babe Ruth (allegedly) when asked why he should be
paid more than U.S. president Herbert Hoover.

New York Yankees spring training camp in St. Petersburg, Florida, in March 1930 was conducted against the backdrop of the early days of the Great Depression. Fortunes had been lost, billions of dollars in assets were wiped out and millions of people were turned out of their jobs. Businessman Arthur A. Robertson told writer Studs Terkel years later, "On Wall Street the people walked around like zombies . . . one of my friends said to me, 'If this keeps going on as they are, we'll all have to go begging.' And I said, 'Who from?'"

As bad as the Depression was that March, few could have forseen the economic misery of the long decade that lay ahead. In the case of George Herman Ruth, the man known to the public as the Babe, the slugging outfielder had no idea there was even an economic crisis going on as he talked about his contract negotiations in the Florida sunshine. "What's that you say?" he asked when told there were bread riots back in his adopted hometown of New York City.

Ruth had become the most famous American of his time. Since showing up in 1914 as an unpolished left-handed pitcher out of the Baltimore workhouses, he was now a household name — whether as the Babe, the Sultan of Swat, the Bambino or the King of Clout. He was a Falstaff who'd revolutionized the national pastime of baseball. With prodigious appetites for home runs, beer, women and attention, he'd been the embodiment of the Roaring Twenties with its soaring stock market and Prohibition parties.

"He was the best baseball player who ever lived," wrote Robert W. Creamer, a Ruth biographer, in a 1995 *Smithsonian* article. "He was better than Ty Cobb, better than Joe DiMaggio, better than Ted Williams, better than Henry Aaron, better than Bobby Bonds. He was by far the most flamboyant. There's never been anyone else like him."

Before Ruth, the home run was an anomaly in baseball.

It was a game of hitting the gaps in the outfield, taking the extra base and sliding with your spikes high. John Franklin Baker got the nickname "Home Run" for hitting just 98 homers over his 14-year career. Baker was a member of the Philadelphia Athletics' "$100,000 Outfield" in the early 1910s. Only a decade later, Ruth would make Baker and his team look quaint. In his transition from successful pitcher to slugging outfielder, the Bambino would change the home-run landscape, setting the single-season record with 29 in 1919. The next year, the Babe was infamously sold by the Boston Red Sox to the New York Yankees for $100,000. Upon joining the Yankees, Ruth exploded with 54 home runs in 1920 and 59 in 1921.

In the world's financial capital, Ruth was the profitable face of his Yankees, leading them to seven American League championships and four World Series championships. He was the prime gate attraction at Yankee Stadium when it opened in 1923 and at the parks he visited with the Yankees and his many barnstorming teams. He was a familiar figure in the newspapers, on the movie screen and on the radios of Americans. It was fair to say that without Ruth, baseball might not have survived the ravages of the Depression intact. Whatever Babe was being paid, it was probably a bargain to Major League Baseball as it sought to navigate the challenging financial times.

As one reporter wrote, "This new fan didn't know where first base was, but he had heard of Babe Ruth and wanted to see him hit a home run. When the Babe hit one, the fan went back the next day and knew not only where first base was, but second base as well."

Not that Ruth's bosses appreciated his value as he

contemplated his new contract offer in 1930. Ruth was coming off a three-year deal that had paid him $70,000 a year. When Yankees owner Colonel Tillinghast L'Hommedieu Huston stated that Ruth was being paid like a railroad president, he must've meant a very small railroad. As Leigh Montville points out in his book *The Big Bam*, for Ruth to be paid the equivalent of the 2005 Alex Rodriguez contract ($25 million per year) in the 1920s, he'd have had to be making $2.25 million. Ruth was still getting much more than any other player, however. When he signed his five-year deal for $52,000 a year in 1922, the next-best contract was for Home Run Baker, who made just $16,000.

Ruth had a lot of lead in his pencil in those 1930 negotiations with the Yankees. While no one had been able to precisely identify how much attendance would drop at Yankee Stadium without the Babe, the number was likely significant — and would become more significant as the Depression wore on. What we do know is that home attendance for all the teams on which Ruth played was 17,959,826. It was at least that much in the cities he visited in the Red Sox or Yankees uniform. Put simply, Ruth's presence turned crowds of a few thousand into tens of thousands. In today's sports economy, that would be a bargaining club with which Ruth could beat the Yankees.

But these were the days before players had agents or lawyers to help them when they went head-to-head with the financial acumen of the businessmen who owned teams. There was no salary disclosure, no public recognition of what a radio contract might pay a team, no shoe deals. It was a matter of faith that owners were giving players true value for their services. Some owners were generous. Others were reasonable. And some, like Chicago White Sox owner Charles Comiskey, were cutthroats who knew their leverage and used it. The underlying cause of the infamous Black Sox scandal — where Chicago players were bribed to throw the 1919 World Series — was the resentment of players who'd been skinned by Comiskey for salaries and bonuses they thought they were owed.

Owners also liked having it both ways. In 1902, a court case involving future Hall of Famer Nap Lajoie illustrates the point. Lajoie was under contract to the National League's Philadelphia Phillies but signed a contract with the American League's Philadelphia Athletics — this during a time when the National League and American League really were two separate leagues. The Phillies sued to prevent Lajoie from breaking his contract and attempted to get an injunction — an order from the court that would force Lajoie to work for the Phillies. Injunctions to force someone to work for another are rarely granted by courts because they are hard to enforce — imagine if a court ordered you to work at a job you just tried to leave (how hard would you work at it?) — and money compensates the employer. In Lajoie's case, he was seen as specially skilled enough; it was acknowledged that although "[h]e may not be the sun in the baseball firmament . . . he is certainly a bright particular star" who could not be replaced.

Now, how irreplaceable was Lajoie? In his contract with the Phillies, as with most, if not all, baseball contracts at the time, the owners could terminate the contract with 10 days' notice. So while Lajoie could not quit the Phillies, they could fire him at will. Little wonder players settled fast and rarely pushed their leverage with owners like Comiskey backed by the flinty new commissioner, Kenesaw Mountain Landis. Negotiating was a one-way proposition.

Ruth was fortunate that the Yankees did not take the scorched-earth approach with him. Left to his own devices, the man with barely a grade-school education negotiated his own contracts using the tools available to him. That meant holding out and leaking stories to friendly writers to make his case in the newspapers. When he signed his first big deal in 1922, after coming over from Boston, he was at odds with Yankees owner Colonel Huston over the annual salary. Huston was offering $50,000 a year. Ruth liked the sound of $1,000 a week, and asked for $52,000. The two men haggled (and drank) until Ruth resolved to end the argument with a coin flip. Huston thought that a sporting proposition. After Huston was given permission to proceed, he flipped a silver half dollar. Ruth said tails. As the coin spun to a stop on the floor of Huston's hotel room in Florida, it came up tails. And thus Ruth was awarded $52,000 a year for five years.

He proved full value for the new contract as he filled Huston's coffers and pushed the Yankees to the beginning of what would be a monumental championship run starting in 1921. The Bronx Bombers won 20 World Series titles in 28 World Series appearances during a run that didn't end till 1964. The numbers he put up during those five seasons have stood the test of time when the claim is made for Babe as the greatest hitter ever. He slammed 194 homers, drove in 570 runs and scored 588 runs. In his contract year of 1926, he hit 47 homers, drove in 153 and scored 139 times in front of Lou Gehrig.

His next contract negotiation came in 1927, just before what many consider the greatest single season by a Major League team — the Murderers' Row of the 1927 Yankees. When the Yankees sought to renew his previous yearly salary of $52,000, Ruth felt compelled to play tough with the team. Ty Cobb was now being paid more than him, Ruth argued through his media surrogates. He sent a demand to the Yankees to be paid $100,000 a year and then headed to Hollywood to make movies and barnstorm across the nation, playing exhibitions and vaudeville shows to raise more money for his lavish lifestyle.

After a whirlwind winter filled with public appearances, Ruth arrived back in New York City to prepare for 1927 spring training. He played tight-lipped about what he might do if he didn't get his desired compensation. The media roiled with speculation. Then, almost as an afterthought, the months of speculation ended quietly in a three-year deal at $70,000 a year, signed days after his arrival in New York. Everyone professed themselves happy, and the Yankees, led by Ruth, won another two World Series titles in 1927 and '28. He hit a record 60 homers (a mark that lasted until 1961) and 165 RBIs in 1927.

By the time the $70,000-a-year deal ended in 1930, there was a little more urgency for a 35-year old Ruth. The big paydays were going to end within a few years for the veteran slugger, and there was no indication the Yankees or anyone else would hire him to manage a team — a long-held desire for Ruth. After years of the

Bambino's larger-than-life personality and oversized ego, the Yankees were growing tired of his act. Illness, suspension, fights with managers, disputes with Commissioner Landis and a casual approach to conditioning meant that he had to now produce at his usual levels or else be faced with being shipped out of town. Again, the Yankees offered no raise, a move that caused Ruth to issue the ultimate public threat a player could use at the time: holdout or retirement.

He wanted $85,000 for three years. Either he got his money or he'd retire, he said in a letter delivered to all the New York sports editors. There was a concession to Father Time in Ruth's attitude about his new contract. "A few years ago I could not take this attitude. I would be obliged to sign at whatever terms for the same reason that 95 percent of all players have to sign — bread and butter . . . well, there is enough bread and butter in our home, even if I do not touch another baseball for the rest of my life."

Ruth's ultimatum began a phony war in the press in which Ruth played the hurt party while the Yankees waited out their man. In previous years, negotiations had always wrapped up in time for Ruth to don his familiar No. 3 and start belting home runs in spring training. In 1930, the possibility of Ruth refusing to play until his contract was done seemed real. The stalemate dragged on until spring training in St. Petersburg. On the eve of the first game, Colonel Jake Ruppert — now handling Ruth's contract negotiations — offered two years at $75;000 per season. Ruth snorted that he would only sign for the $85,000-a-year figure he'd told the press. To back up the threat, he told writer Dan Daniel (one of several ghost writers used by Ruth) that he would not wear the Yankees jersey against Boston the next day unless he got his way.

As Daniel told the story (or embellished it to suit his purposes), he had become convinced that the optics of Ruth holding out for so much money as the Depression raged would be bad for the Babe. He reminded Ruth there'd been riots in New York City over the dire state of the economy. According to Daniel, Ruth professed ignorance of the suffering of many of his fans. Chastened, Ruth headed over to Ruppert's hotel in time to settle for the two years at $80,000 a year. The only concession he wrestled from the Yankees was the return of $5,000 in fines he'd paid under manager Miller Huggins for various infringements of team rules.

Getting $80,000 in 1930 was nothing to sneeze at for a 35-year-old athlete staring squarely the end of his career. Using the leverage they held over him, the Yankees could have ground him down to their original offer or lower. With his baseball income augmented by his many other endeavors, Ruth was well off by any measure and would remain so if he could curb his gambling habits. So while many of his teammates retired without notice or a final payday, Ruth was given a farewell tour — one that lasted another four seasons.

There was only one more World Series title in Ruth's tenure in the Bronx, but he happily pounded out 40-plus homers a year in concert with Lou Gehrig, who batted right behind him. When injuries finally slowed him down in 1934, Ruth hoped to stay on as the Yankees manager — as a sign of respect for his contributions over the years. But the Yankees dumped him off to the Boston Braves as a player/coach. The playing aspect ended just a few weeks into the 1935 season. Ruth, unhappy in Boston, didn't finish out the year. He tried a coaching gig with the Brooklyn Dodgers in 1938, but that too was a failure; he wanted to be manager, not a subordinate. Ruth was always a headline entertainer. He retired from the field with a whimper, not his traditional bang.

The business of being the Babe would consume him until his death in 1948. Still, Ruth's impact on baseball went past his exploits on the field. Ruth had shown his fellow players that there was serious money to be made in baseball, even in the worst economic times of the century. All it took was leverage. In Babe's case, that leverage was enormous talent fueled by a supportive New York press corps. It probably couldn't have happened had Ruth been the best player of all time in Cincinnati or Pittsburgh. While his compensation was more like that of the owner of a modest railroad, it was still more money than most of the green country boys who played the game could hope to see in 10 lifetimes.

Baseball's owners had been watching Ruth's spiraling salary, too. Even if it wasn't a king's ransom like those enjoyed by today's athletes, it was still cause for concern. The Yankees might have been able to pay such salaries with the revenues from their market, but other owners could not do the same in what was then still very much a regional sport. It was hardly a coincidence that no baseball player approached Ruth's levels of compensation until the 1960s.

In ensuring that Ruth's contractual largesse would not be matched for decades, Major League Baseball was aided by a legal decision that was reached just as Ruth started putting up his mammoth home-run numbers in the early 1920s. More than Ruth's salary demands, a case known as *Federal Baseball Club v. National League* defined baseball's financial landscape for over half a century. It was launched by the owners of the Federal League's Baltimore Terrapins against the National League and the American League for conspiring to monopolize baseball by destroying the Federal League.

While other teams in the Federal League had been compensated when the Federal League folded (one bought into the Chicago Cubs and moved them to Wrigley Field), the Terrapins had been left out. So they sued under the provisions of the *Sherman* and *Clayton* antitrust acts, claiming that baseball was violating antitrust laws. At trial, the defendants were found jointly liable, with damages of $80,000 assessed. The figure was tripled to $240,000 under antitrust law's "treble-damages" award. Baseball owners appealed, and the District of Columbia Court of Appeals reversed the decision, finding that baseball was not a monopoly. From there, it made its way to the Supreme Court of the United States.

Just as Ruth was making his name, the Supreme Court of the day was full of eminent legal personalities. Chief Justice William Taft (who was U.S. president from 1909 to 1913, and the first sitting president to throw out an Opening Day pitch), Oliver Wendell Holmes Jr., Louis Brandeis and Joseph McKenna were among those on the bench that heard the case. The issue was framed as whether baseball constituted interstate commerce or whether it was simply a set of intrastate businesses exempt from antitrust legislation. While the sport conducted itself in a number of states, lawyers for the two baseball leagues argued that their business did not constitute interstate commerce like a railway or steel company's business did.

The case was heard in April 1922, just as Ruth was coming off his record 59-homer season. The decision came only six weeks later, on May 29, 1922. In what was probably not a surprise to many in the game, baseball had prevailed in a unanimous decision. Justice Holmes wrote: "The business is giving exhibitions of baseball, which are purely state affairs. It is true that, in order to attain for these exhibitions the great popularity that they have achieved, competitions must be arranged between clubs from different cities and states. But the fact that, in order to give the exhibitions, the Leagues must induce free persons to cross state lines and must arrange and pay for their doing so is not enough to change the character of the business."

Holmes compared baseball teams traveling to other cities to "a firm of lawyers sending out a member to argue a case, or the Chautauqua lecture bureau sending out lecturers," which "does not engage in such commerce because the lawyer or lecturer goes to another state." And with that, baseball had a blank check to operate as it wished for the next 50 years, interpreting contracts and labor statutes as it saw fit, without government interference. The impact on players was that workplace issues and salary disputes were adjudicated by the commissioner of baseball, who was bought and paid for by the owners. He interpreted the reserve clause as binding a player in perpetuity to a club, despite the player having fulfilled the terms of his contract.

It didn't hurt that presidents and politicians in Congress were baseball fans in this period, disinclined to upset the fantasy world of sports. Plus the decision was rendered in the aftermath of the "Black Sox" betting scandal in the 1919 World Series, which tainted baseball and its players for many. Granting players any advantages after the disgrace of Eddie Cicotte, Buck Weaver, "Shoeless" Joe Jackson and the five other Chicago players involved in the betting scheme might have been a bit much for the public of the times.

The decision had long-lasting effects, and a 1953 challenge by a player named George Toolson was similarly spiked by the court, with a 7–2 decision upholding the original 1922 judgment. The issue of a player's right to determine where and how he wanted to play wouldn't receive a full rehearing until 1969, when Curt Flood, the All-Star center fielder of the St. Louis Cardinals, launched a brave but ultimately futile reairing of the same issues settled by the Holmes decision in Babe Ruth's heyday.

1.2 CURT FLOOD

Curt Flood had every reason to be content in 1969. The three-time All-Star and seven-time Gold Glove center fielder was making $90,000 a year to play baseball. Yes, he'd just been traded by the St. Louis Cardinals, who had won the 1967 World Series and made the World Series in 1968, to the woeful Philadelphia Phillies. But he still had years left in his career to reestablish himself in another city. He had fame, an art business and a wide circle of friends inside and outside the sport. He was also a leader on racial issues within baseball.

But Flood was deeply upset by how he'd been treated by the Cardinals, for whom he'd starred since 1958. He felt he'd been treated like a piece of meat and likened baseball's lifetime hold on his destiny to slavery. In a time when racial enlightenment was becoming a major societal factor in America — the *Civil Rights Act* having been recently passed by Congress in 1964 — Flood's words hit home. When people said, "$90,000 a year is a lot of money for a slave," Flood fired back, "A well-paid slave is still a slave."

Flood had become a troublesome employee for the Cardinals in the final year of his contract. He was noisily demanding $100,000 in his next deal. He was increasingly outspoken about civil rights in baseball. His brother had been arrested for robbing a jewelry store, and Flood was drinking too much. When the Cardinals found a buyer for Flood in Philadelphia, they were happy to get him out of town.

At issue was not principally the money in Flood's contract. It was, as he liked to say, his freedom. The fleet outfielder had played out the terms of his previous contract with St. Louis. With the contract expired, Flood contended that the Cardinals had no right to trade his rights to the Phillies. He should have been a free agent to do what he pleased. What he pleased was to stay in St. Louis or else go to a city of his choice. But in MLB, protected by its antitrust exemption from the Supreme Court, athletes were bound by the insidious device known as the reserve clause.

Since 1879, teams in the various baseball leagues had agreed that they could "reserve" players, free from tampering or competition from other teams. The reserve clause provided the team a unilateral option to negotiate with the player in the future. As NHL Players' Association director Alan Eagleson, who was a close ally to owners instead of his players (we'll talk about his fraud charges later), testified in the Flood case: "[The reserve clause] is considered by me, and I am sure by most, to be simply a lifetime option clause and that a player once he signs the contract, since that is the standard contract of the league, signs with a team for life." Therefore, if you were a player, you were prevented from ever negotiating with another team, as the team you'd played for retained control of your playing rights until it saw fit to trade them.

The reserve clause had been subjected to various legal challenges long before Curt Flood came along. One of the first came from baseball player Hal Chase in 1914. Chase tried to leave the American League's Chicago White Sox and join a team in the Federal League. Chicago sought an injunction from the court to stop him. In its decision, the court refused to grant an injunction on two grounds. First, the court found that the contract lacked "mutuality." Generally, a contract should be arrived at through a fair negotiation between the parties. In this case, where Chase could not leave the White Sox but the White Sox could terminate Chase's contract with 10 days' notice, the court found the contract to lack this basic mutuality. Second, the court found that, although baseball may not be subject to federal law (a precursor to the "antitrust exemption" granted to baseball by the U.S. Supreme Court in 1922), awarding an injunction would only promote a monopoly in player services and would stifle personal liberty.

Another player, Danny Gardella, had sued Major League Baseball in 1947, challenging the *Federal Baseball Club v. National League* decision. He had ammunition, in the trial decision, Judge Jerome Frank had written that the reserve clause "results in something resembling peonage" and "possesses characteristics shockingly repugnant to moral principles." But Gardella settled for $60,000, and the merits of the case were never heard by the Supreme Court.

The reserve clause was next tested unsuccessfully in court by George Toolson in 1953. Justice William O. Douglas (who would also hear the Flood case years later) upheld the 1922 decision; Justices Harold Hitz Burton and Stanley Forman Reed dissented, saying baseball as it was then played met the definition of interstate commerce. The judges who heard the case took the opinion that only the U.S. Congress could act to end baseball's antitrust exemption granted by the court 30 years before. But congressmen saw no upside to disturbing the national pastime. It would be another 19 years before the issue would be considered again.

Flood was going against decades of inaction, precedent and misconception about the free market for players when he told the Phillies he wouldn't report to training camp in 1970. No wonder Dick Allen — a quixotic figure himself in his career — shook his head in amazement about the man he'd been traded for that winter. "Curt Flood? My hat's off to him," said Allen. "I think he's all man, that 160 pounds."

For all his determination, Flood's epic decision might never have gone anywhere had it not been for another notable figure: Marvin Miller. Miller, the executive director of the MLB Players Association, was a man as determined as Curt Flood to change baseball's monopoly. Miller had assumed the mantle of a toothless, underfunded MLBPA in 1965. As a former executive of the United Steelworkers Union, he was steeped in classic labor politics. The diminutive, mustachioed Miller was determined to make the MLBPA a viable bargaining threat for owners. Even as players themselves questioned Miller's moves, he put the owners on notice. In short order, he created a revenue stream for the players and the union through the selling of trading-card rights. But after years of butting heads in the steel industry, he had no illusions that baseball's cantankerous owners would be pushovers.

Flood would prove to be the man to promote Miller's cherished philosophy that players deserved freedom to negotiate the terms of their employment. But first he had to test Flood. When the two men first met in New York City to discuss Flood's challenge, Miller did everything he could to discourage Flood from challenging the reserve clause. He reminded Flood that a challenge going to the Supreme Court would take up to three years and that his career was likely over if he chose that course. He asked him if he had enough money to sustain himself over that time. Miller also asked Flood if he had any skeletons in his closet that could be used against him by owners. He told Flood that he'd have to convince his fellow players in the union that he was serious and not just looking for handout money from them.

Finally, Miller told Flood the odds of the U.S. Supreme Court's reversing itself were very slim. Yes, many of the conditions cited in the *Federal Baseball Club v. National League* opinion had changed — television, interstate commerce and labor law rendered much of the old logic moot. In fact, the U.S. Supreme Court denied an antitrust exemption to the NFL in *Radovich v. NFL* — a decision that spent paragraphs reiterating how *Federal Baseball Club v. National League* was wrongly decided and stating "that, were we considering the question of baseball for the first time upon a clean slate, we would have no doubts" that baseball would be subject to antitrust laws. But the principle of *stare decisis* (letting a decision stand) was a powerful factor in Supreme Court decisions. As Miller recounted in his memoir, he told Flood that "given the courts' history of bias towards the owners and their monopoly, he didn't have a chance in hell of winning. More important than that, I told him even if he won, he'd never get anything out of it — he'd never get a job in baseball again." Flood assured him on all counts — he was in.

Baseball was unimpressed. The new MLB commissioner Bowie Kuhn tried a fatherly approach to what he clearly saw as a misguided young man. He attempted to make nice with Flood. The patrician Kuhn was quickly rebuffed. Astonished at Flood's impertinence, Kuhn then tried to intimidate the player by putting him on baseball's suspended list, making him ineligible to play until he dropped his demands and reported to the Phillies. Flood never blinked. Through their media outlets, the owners claimed Flood was a stooge for Miller. Flood shrugged and issued a letter to Bowie Kuhn that rings with clarity to this day.

December 24, 1969

After twelve years in the major leagues, I do not
feel I am a piece of property to be bought and sold
irrespective of my wishes. I believe that any system
which produces that result violates my basic rights
as a citizen and is inconsistent with the laws of the
United States and of the several States.

It is my desire to play baseball in 1970, and I
am capable of playing. I have received a contract
offer from the Philadelphia club, but I believe I
have the right to consider offers from other clubs
before making any decision. I, therefore, request
that you make known to all Major League clubs
my feelings in this matter, and advise them of my
availability for the 1970 season.

The first step was for Flood to request a preliminary
injunction to have his trade from St. Louis ruled illegal
on the grounds that the reserve clause harmed Flood's
constitutional rights. If this Hail Mary worked, he might
be restored to the Cardinals' roster in time for the 1970
season. If it failed, he knew that the MLB owners would
blackball him, and he might never see a playing field again
in the majors.

Miller chose a man he knew well to lead the attack
on MLB's antitrust exemption: former Supreme Court
justice and U.S. secretary of labor Arthur Goldberg —
who was simultaneously running for governor of New
York State. While MLB played down the significance of
the hearing on the injunction, legendary sports journalists

such as Howard Cosell and Dave Anderson knew better. They were in the front rows as testimony began. "A great day for the scribes," Cosell kept repeating as he strolled the courtroom. The other major professional team sports leagues also understood that a win by Flood would massively affect them all, and they were interested spectators as well.

There was little chance that Judge Irving Ben Cooper would find for Flood against 50 years of Supreme Court precedence. In practice, only the Supreme Court could overturn its own work. Plus, Cooper was clearly impressed by the majesty of the MLB luminaries in his court, lined up by Commissioner Kuhn. It would come as no surprise when he later concluded, "The game is on higher ground; it behooves every one to keep it there."

During the injunction hearing, Cooper kept a tight rein on Flood's legal team. When his decision was announced to deny the injunction, there was no surprise from anyone except, perhaps, Flood. But Cooper also wrote that there was sufficient reason to proceed with a separate case testing baseball's reserve clause. "For years baseball players have chafed under the restrictions of baseball's reserve system . . . many of them appear justified." Cooper ordered a full trial in just six short weeks, with himself as the presiding judge.

While the two sides prepared for the showdown in court, Kuhn brokered a deal between the Cardinals and Phillies, allowing the trade to go through, with Willie Montanez and Jim Browning going to Philadelphia instead of Flood. Flood meanwhile received financial backing from the MLBPA and from writing a magazine article for *Sport*.

But he was clearly upset, knowing that he would not play in 1970 or any other year until he won the case or agreed to the trade to Philadelphia (which upped its salary offer to almost $100,000 behind the scenes).

He must have also known that former players or executives would not likely testify on his behalf about the reserve clause — not if they wanted another job in baseball. Baseball owners were a vindictive breed. In January 1970, Flood announced his lawsuit against the antitrust provisions in New York City, where MLB was headquartered, with the trial scheduled to begin on May 19. Flood would ask for one million dollars in his lawsuit against Kuhn and Major League Baseball, alleging a violation of federal antitrust laws.

Because time was short and Goldberg was campaigning for the New York governor's job, both sides were barely prepared for such a monumental case. A very nervous and poorly prepared Flood was the first witness. He had trouble remembering details of his career and contract negotiations. The defense was forced to introduce one of Flood's playing cards to get a record of his career. Cooper constantly admonished him to speak up.

For all his shortcomings as a witness, Flood repeated his unequivocal message: a well-paid slave is still a slave; every player should have the right to a free market. When pressed by MLB's lawyer Mark Hughes on how he would remedy the ills of the reserve clause, Flood stated the (then radical) notion that "I would like the whole system to be struck down and declared illegal." The defense lawyers thought this boxed in Flood to a solution that almost everyone at the time thought impractical: MLB and its union negotiating a system for free agency. Most of the writers in attendance agreed; Flood hadn't helped his case.

Things went better with Flood's next witness: the great Jackie Robinson. Though suffering from the diabetes that would prematurely end his life at 53, the man who broke baseball's color barrier was an impressive figure. While almost everyone else in baseball who might have agreed with Flood on the reserve clause was cowed by the owners, Robinson was fearless as he discussed the careers of fine players on great teams who were buried in the minors behind star players, unable to move to a team where they might make a better dollar. "Anything that is one-sided in this country is wrong," he told the court. "And I think the reserve clause is a one-sided thing in favor of the owners." Robinson added the prescient comment, "I think unless there is a change in the reserve clause that it is going to lead to a serious strike in terms of the ballplayers." (Cooper was so impressed by Robinson that he asked him to his chambers to autograph a baseball for his grandson.)

The great Tigers slugger Hank Greenberg, who'd been a player and a manager in the majors, also testified against the reserve clause. Despite being the greatest Tigers slugger ever (and the greatest Jewish major leaguer prior to Sandy Koufax), he had been unceremoniously dumped by Detroit to Pittsburgh after serving four years in World War II on active duty. Greenberg's $75,000 salary was too rich for Detroit, which sent him to the lowly Pirates for the waiver price of $10,000. Greenberg, like Robinson, talked about players he'd seen buried in the minors by the reserve clause, robbed of their best earning years.

A businessman himself, Greenberg urged negotiation on the reserve clause between owners and players.
"It seems to me that the times have changed," he told the
court. "And that the owners and the players are going to
have to get together and work more harmoniously and
with a major cooperative spirit so that the game can go
forward." Cooper asked him what was wrong about the
reserve clause. "It's a unilateral contract, Judge. The player
has no choice other than to accept the terms offered to
him." Although it had no effect on the decision, Cooper
praised Greenberg's lucid testimony. "That is really the
sort of thing I seek," Cooper told him.

Flood's team also produced the free-spirited Chicago
White Sox owner, Bill Veeck, to support the claims against
the reserve clause. Veeck was an anomaly: a showman
who thought baseball should be fun. Naturally, the other
owners loathed him for his promotions (outfield fences
that moved back and forth during games) and experi-
ments (he sent a dwarf to bat for Cleveland in a major-
league game; the dwarf walked on four pitches, and the
commissioner banned dwarves). "Everyone should once
in their business career have the right to determine their
future for themselves," Veeck told Cooper. He said the
reserve clause was "human bondage." The one-legged
Veeck (he'd lost his leg as a marine in World War II) urged
MLB and the players to negotiate a compromise on the
reserve clause. He suggested several alternatives that have
proven farsighted half a century later. Naturally, Cooper
found him a bit much and discredited his evidence.

When it came time for MLB to mount its defense,
it hauled out the big hitters from other sports. NFL

commissioner Pete Rozelle, NBA commissioner J. Walter Kennedy, economist Robert Nathan and NHL Players' Association director Eagleson (always a friend to owners) were among those to testify that, without the reserve clause, teams would disappear, leagues would collapse and the hot dogs at games might not taste as good. That also produced a series of baseball owners who said they would not have bought teams if not for the certainty afforded them by the reserve clause. Ewing Kauffman, who'd built a pharmaceutical empire, best illustrated the mindset of owners as he described the value of the reserve clause to his business. When he was asked by Flood's lawyer Jay Topkis how much he would pay for Flood's services. Kauffman did not hesitate: $125,000 a year, he said — maybe more if he could get him on a multiyear contract. In that moment, Kauffman illustrated why players wanted the reserve clause gone and why owners like Kauffman needed it to prevent players from getting true market value.

The reserve clause was always an easy sell to the public. Not only did the owners believe in the sanctity of the reserve clause, so did most of the fans, and not a few of the athletes themselves. Having had a half century of the clause, most could not conceive of another system that wouldn't produce the rich teams holding all the best players. In the Gardella case, Hall of Famers Stan Musial, Bob Feller and even banned Black Sox pitcher Eddie Cicotte warned about the perils to competition of abandoning the reserve clause. A poll that year said that 69 percent of Americans thought it necessary to keep it.

Commissioner Kuhn summed up the owners' position. Summoning his best rhetorical flair, Kuhn proclaimed that "baseball as we know it would not survive" without the right to bind players permanently to their last contracted team. He compared the MLB of 1970 to the chaotic baseball landscape of a century earlier, when leagues and teams folded every season. He was right about one thing regarding the 1870s and its Gilded Age — that was where the attitudes of his owners still resided.

If Flood needed an indication of which way the wind was blowing, he needed only see Judge Cooper praising NFL commissioner Pete Rozelle's skills as a witness. "Very good. You handled yourself well. I compliment you." When the testimony in the case ended, not one current MLB player had testified or even presented himself in court to watch. Miller, who rarely erred or admitted to a mistake, said that not getting players to at least attend had been his biggest mistake. But he did make a significant gain for players even as the Flood trial proceeded. He helped negotiate the 1970 Basic Agreement, covering many conditions of players' employment — including the right to independent arbitration of grievances. From that day on in baseball, said writer Dick Young, Kuhn was a figurehead: the owners "have peddled away his power. They have conceded, at last, that he is their commissioner, not the players' commissioner."

In August 1970, Cooper issued a 47-page decision in which he wrote, "Clearly, the preponderance of the credible proof does not favor elimination of the reserve clause." In fact, Cooper had to admit that, despite ordering the trial, he had no right to overturn the Supreme Court decision of 1922. Finally, he took a jab at Flood's claim to indentured servitude. There was nothing, wrote Cooper, that prevented Flood from getting a job outside baseball.

Cooper's decision ultimately pleased no one, because both Flood's team and the owners saw it as a step on the way to an eventual Supreme Court challenge.

Flood's team was not dismayed by Cooper's work. "Judge Cooper only held that it was up to the Supreme Court to overrule the Supreme Court," said Marvin Miller. The next step on the road to having the Supreme Court hear Flood's case was to appeal to the Second Circuit Court of Appeals, which affirmed Cooper's decision on the basis of the 1922 Supreme Court decision. One of the three justices on the Second Circuit noted that, based on *stare decisis*, he thought it unlikely the Supreme Court would overturn the decision.

The MLBPA didn't disagree, and though Flood himself was succumbing to the pressure of public scrutiny, they vowed to move forward. As the case wound its way toward the eventual U.S. Supreme Court hearing, Flood decided to take a final shot at regaining his baseball career — and earning the money that he desperately needed after having no MLB income since 1969. It was arranged for him to launch a comeback with the Washington Senators, then managed by the immortal Ted Williams. The Senators owner, Bob Short, gambled on using Flood as a drawing card in the predominately black city of Washington, DC. He offered Flood a $110,000 salary, an offer Flood couldn't refuse. But the year away from baseball and Flood's drinking problems doomed the comeback. He quit just a few weeks into the season, sending his teammates a note saying, "I tried year and a half is too much very serious personal problems mounting."

Now all that remained of his lifetime attachment to

the game was his quixotic case. Early on, it seemed that the case would not garner the necessary votes from the Supreme Court to even be considered for an open hearing. It needed four votes of the nine-person panel, which had just added Lewis Powell and William Rehnquist to replace two deceased members. But months passed without any indication from the justices' deliberations that they would take up the case that would become *Flood v. Kuhn*. Then, for no appreciable reason, the court granted *certiorari,* setting the way for oral arguments on March 20, 1972 (Justice Powell recused himself from the case because he owned stock in Anheuser-Busch, which owned the Cardinals).

Most of the arguments from the preliminary injunction hearing had been refined by the two sides in the interim. The owners' lawyers continued to stress the mythical place baseball had in the life of the country at the time. They also put forth the idea that the reserve clause was something to be negotiated with the union and should come under the jurisdiction of the Department of Labor. And they contended that Flood was merely a prop in a suit brought by the union.

The Flood team had planned to argue that the conditions governing the interstate commerce of baseball in 1922 no longer applied. Further, the court had refused to extend baseball's antitrust exemption to the NFL, NBA or NHL. Finally, it would argue, as Flood had, "I do not feel I am a piece of property to be bought and sold irrespective of my wishes."

The problem was that Flood's lawyer Goldberg, the former Supreme Court justice, had not prepared properly for the presentation to his former colleagues. His gubernatorial challenge to Nelson Rockefeller had failed, and he was now regretting having left the court at the behest of Lyndon Johnson to become ambassador to the United Nations a half decade prior. When he came to present to the justices, he got Flood's biography incorrect, left the discussion of labor law until he'd used up all but one minute of his limited time and was upbraided by the justices for misallocating his time.

One story the Flood team had prepared to present was that of Vida Blue, the 22-year-old Oakland A's pitcher who won both the Cy Young Award and the AL Most Valuable Player in 1971. When he asked for a raise from $14,750 to $92,000, his owner, Charlie Finley, threatened to trade him or blackball him. As a result, Blue announced his retirement. It took Commissioner Kuhn's intervention to win Blue a $63,000 salary. Blue's very contemporary example would have buttressed Flood's argument about the unfairness of the reserve clause. But Goldberg did not mention Blue, instead droning on about Flood's career statistics (a lifetime batting average of .293 with 1,861 hits, 85 home runs, 851 runs and 636 RBI) to the bored justices. When he sat down, the justices asked him no further questions to spare him further embarrassment.

When MLB's legal counsel Lou Hoynes came to argue on behalf of the owners, he was forced to admit that baseball was indeed commerce. But he reiterated that the issues at stake were properly part of collective bargaining, not a legal challenge. (Hoynes neglected to mention the 12-day strike by players at the start of the 1972 season as proof that collective bargaining was the proper route for amending the reserve clause.) The frustrated justices tried to get Hoynes to address why baseball should keep its exemption while other sports were denied the same. But Hoynes deflected the arguments.

While waiting for the outcome, Flood retreated to Europe to escape mounting debts and problems with alcohol. He was in Spain when the 5–3 decision to deny his appeal came down on June 19, 1972. Justice Harry Blackmun wrote the majority decision of *Flood v. Kuhn*. To those who'd speculated that the court would overturn its previous decision, part 1 of Blackmun's decision removed any doubt. In a segment that has become an embarrassment to the court since it was issued, Blackmun wrote a sentimental paean to the sport, listing the names of 83 famous players and recalling the lines of the poem "Casey at the Bat." The syrupy ode was such an embarrassment that Chief Justice Warren Burger and Justice Byron White, two of the justices who voted with the majority, declined to approve it.

When Justice Blackmun finally got around to the bones of the case, he admitted that the game had changed: "it seems appropriate now to say that: Professional baseball is a business and engaged in interstate commerce." Invoking the Radovich decision that failed to extend antitrust exemption to the NFL, he wrote, "the slate is not clean. Indeed it has not been clean for half a century." The antitrust exemption created in *Federal Baseball* and upheld in *Toolson* was "an aberration confined to baseball."

But Blackmun was concerned about the turmoil that ending the reserve clause would cause his beloved baseball. "Even though others might regard this as 'unrealistic, inconsistent, or illogical,' the aberration is an established one." Therefore it behooved the justices to allow it to stand. "Under these circumstances, there is merit in consistency, even though some might claim that beneath that consistency is a layer of inconsistency." Clearly, Justice Blackmun and the concurring justices were tossing the issue back to Congress. Since Congress had shown no desire in 50 years to change the law, *stare decisis* should apply.

In the dissenting opinion, Justice William O. Douglas, who had voted to perpetuate the exemption in *Toolson*, now had second thoughts. He called the original *Federal Baseball* decision of 1922 a "derelict in the stream of law that we, its creator, should remove. Only a romantic view of a rather dismal business account over the last 50 years would keep that derelict in midstream." Douglas agreed with Flood that the reserve clause unlawfully benefited the owners at players' expense:

> Baseball is today big business that is packaged with beer, with broadcasting, and with other industries. The beneficiaries of the *Federal Baseball Club* decision are not the Babe Ruths, Ty Cobbs and Lou Gehrigs. The owners, whose records many say reveal a proclivity for predatory practices, do not come to us with equities. The equities are with the victims of the reserve clause. I use the word "victims" in the Sherman Act sense, since a contract which forbids anyone to practice his calling is commonly called an unreasonable restraint of trade . . . The unbroken silence of Congress should not prevent us from correcting our own mistakes.

Justice Thurgood Marshall also dissented:

Perhaps we become so enamored of athletics
that we assume that they are foremost in the
minds of legislators as well as fans. We must
not forget, however, that there are only some six
hundred major league baseball players. Whatever
muscle they might have been able to muster by
combining forces with other athletes has been
greatly impaired by the manner in which this
Court has isolated them. It is this Court that
has made them impotent, and this Court should
correct its error . . . Baseball should be covered
by the antitrust laws beginning with this case and
henceforth, unless Congress decides otherwise.

While Flood and Miller had both known going in
that their case was a longshot, the decision to protect the
owners of baseball at the expense of players still stung. By
this time, Flood was broke and moving about Europe to
stay ahead of creditors and the IRS. His knew his career
was over after the aborted comeback with the Senators.
"It would be difficult to come back. And besides, I don't
think I'll be getting the opportunity to play again. As big
as it is, baseball is a closely-knit unit. I doubt even one of
the 24 men controlling the game would touch me with a
10-foot pole. You can't buck the Establishment." He never
held a full-time position in baseball again before his death
in 1997 at the age of 59.

But his contribution to changing baseball and pro
sports in general lives on. While MLB initially celebrated

winning *Flood v. Kuhn,* it was a short-lived respite from reality. The owners' chief negotiator, John Gaherin, looked at the decision and stated, "It wasn't a question of if the reserve clause would be restructured, but when." Flood's legal gamble, once questioned by many players, galvanized the union over the next two decades, making the MLBPA one of the strongest unions in North America. Miller knew that Flood's contribution to the psyche of players who'd been abandoned for so long was vast. *Flood v. Kuhn* raised "the consciousness of everyone involved in baseball: the writers, the fans, the players — and perhaps even some of the owners."

By 1970, owners had negotiated a collective agreement with the players that, while it didn't grant meaningful free agency, did give the players the right to a number of things, including independent arbitration of grievances. A further collective agreement in 1973 provided for salary arbitration. The significance of the 1970 agreement would be seen only three short years after Blackmun's sappy tribute to baseball in *Flood v. Kuhn.* The Catfish Hunter and Andy Messersmith arbitrations that we'll discuss below were only possible from collective bargaining.

The lawsuit also helped swing the major press figures of the day from mocking Flood's "slavery" claim to wholeheartedly supporting their players' fight for rights against the owners. From the time of Flood's suit, a number of prominent voices in the media broke ranks with MLB to support the players in their struggle.

Baseball would undergo eight labor disruptions through 1994, when owners finally realized the futility of trying to force a salary cap on players. The game has had relative labor peace ever since. In 1992, Flood was given the NAACP Jackie Robinson Award for contributions to black athletes, and in 1994, he gave a speech on solidarity to the players as they prepared to go on the strike that canceled that year's World Series. The players reportedly gave him a standing ovation — almost 25 years to the day since he had announced his suit against baseball.

Flood's legacy was later acknowledged in 1997 via the House of Representatives' *Baseball Fans and Communities Protection Act* of 1997. (The act carried Flood's uniform No. 21 — HR 21.) The legislation gave the same antitrust law protection to Major League Baseball players that is provided for other professional athletes. The act was renamed the *Curt Flood Act* and became law in 1998.

1.3 CATFISH HUNTER

For all the attention lavished on *Flood v. Kuhn,* the case did not materially benefit baseball players or any other professional sports athletes facing the reserve clause. Much to Flood's dismay, getting rid of the reserve clause was not part of the 1970 collective agreement negotiated by Marvin Miller between the owners and players. The three-year agreement contained standards for pensions, spring training, moving expenses and a number of items. But nothing about getting rid of the reserve clause.

For all the boldness of the MLBPA's Supreme Court challenge, Miller believed in an incremental approach to equality in collective bargaining with the owners. For the time being, a loud shot across the bows was enough.

Besides, Miller had obtained one other concession in the 1970 talks. He noted that the owners had insisted throughout *Flood v. Kuhn* that the reserve clause should be collectively bargained, not settled in courts. Miller put them to the test. If the owners now refused to bargain on the issue, they'd find themselves in trouble with the National Labor Relations Board for bargaining in bad faith.

Such was the owners' concern about giving up the bigger issue of free agency that they willingly conceded independent arbitration to the players instead. Before this time, the commissioner had had the final say in all arbitration matters. Needless to say, this resulted in players having a very poor batting average when it came to justice on salary and contractual complaints. Now, players with two consecutive years of service or three years of non-consecutive service could appeal their contract offers.

MLB commissioner Bowie Kuhn was not happy with the concession, but Miller made the case that if Kuhn were the arbitrator, he could not be the commissioner of all baseball. Only by standing back from such duties, Miller told him, could Kuhn still pretend that he was the even-handed man concerned with the welfare of the entire sport. Such was Kuhn's vanity that he agreed with Miller's logic. One clause in the new collective bargaining agreement (CBA) specifically said that unless owners rectified missed payments on a contract within 10 days, the player would be declared a free agent. Besides, what could come of it? Kuhn hadn't given up the reserve clause and opened the doors to free agency, and that was the important thing.

It didn't take long for Kuhn to be disabused of such

fantasies. The chain of events that began with establishing an independent arbitration system would, within three years, produce a revolution in free agency that would make baseball players free agents in a real sense. The catalysts were a stubborn owner by the name of Charles O. Finley, owner of the Oakland A's, and a stubborn tobacco farmer from North Carolina with the handle of Jim "Catfish" Hunter.

In the mid-70s, Hunter was the best starting pitcher on the best team in baseball — Finley's Oakland A's. The A's had just won their second of three straight World Series titles in the fall of 1973. Hunter was a major reason Oakland had become a dominant team. He had led the American League in Earned Run Average while winning 21 games in each of 1972 and 1973, for the bargain price of $75,000 per year. There was every reason for Finley to be happy with Hunter, whom he'd personally given the nickname Catfish.

That was important, because not much about paying baseball players made Charlie Finley happy. The Chicago-based insurance executive had purchased the Kansas City Athletics in 1960, dressed them in softball outfits, changed their nickname to the A's and then moved them to Oakland when Kansas City refused to build him a new stadium. Whether in Kansas City or Oakland, Finley ran a tight ship. His wife worked on the team payroll, and there were few frills around the club's operation.

Finley might have run himself out of baseball (Kuhn called him "the village idiot") had it not been for his uncanny ability to find players like Hunter, Reggie Jackson, Vida Blue, Rollie Fingers, Sal Bando and the rest of his championship roster. There was nothing flukey about the A's, who'd beaten the Dodgers and the Reds in consecutive World Series. Hunter was their lynchpin, winning and saving games in the postseason. Letting him get away would be ill-advised. "When we started winning in Oakland, Cat was the father of those teams," Hall of Famer Reggie Jackson said.

At first, it seemed that Finley had avoided losing Hunter. The top salary in baseball that year was Dick Allen's $250,000. Heading into the 1974 season, Hunter had agreed to a two-year deal at $100,000 per year with Finley. The only wrinkle was that Hunter wanted half the money each year deferred into an insurance policy he'd designate for Finley. Maybe Finley was giddy at getting Hunter so cheap — or maybe he wasn't listening carefully — but he said sure to the insurance scheme. To get his tax ducks in a row, Hunter's lawyer, J. Carlton Cherry, ran the plan by the IRS, which approved the concept.

What followed this agreement was a summer-long stall from Finley. Despite repeated letters from Cherry trying to finalize the deal, Finley did what MLB owners had always done — fall back on the commissioner to bail him out if the player got too pushy. His excuses were many. He said that the plan he'd agreed to was not like one he'd done with Reggie Jackson, deferring money (in Jackson's deal Finley controlled the money till Jackson retired; Hunter's was to be paid in 1974 into the insurance policy, denying Finley the chance to use the money), as if one had anything to do with the other.

Finley also said his now-estranged wife, the club's comptroller, refused to sign the contract. He said that

Hunter hadn't delivered the contract on time. In mid-September, as Hunter was leading the A's to their third consecutive World Series title, Cherry put Finley on notice that unless he did what he was supposed to do under the terms of the contract, Hunter would ask to be declared a free agent under the new CBA.

The brewing dispute was music to Miller, who'd been biding his time since the CBA, trying to find a case under the new arbitration system that might result in a free agency for a player. He thought he had a case in 1972 when the St. Louis Cardinals let their young star Ted Simmons play half a season without a contract. The Cardinals had been willing to roll the dice on Simmons, until MLB lawyers advised them that this wasn't the best time to test the reserve clause in court. Simmons played well enough to be a reserve for the 1972 National League All-Star team and had gotten his contract with a healthy raise.

But Finley was not listening to anyone. He was used to having his way under baseball's one-way labor highway. It wasn't until almost a month after Cherry's ultimatum that he realized he wasn't in Kansas City any longer. On the day before Hunter started in the AL Championship Series, Catfish was called into a meeting with Finley. The tip that this was more than a friendly chat was the presence of AL president Lee MacPhail. Finley tried offering Hunter a check for $50,000 on the spot to make things right.

Hunter said the money was not to go to him but to the insurance policy. He left without taking it. "Charlie said, 'Here's the money,'" Hunter told the Associated Press in a 1994 interview. "I told him, 'I don't want it that way. Pay the insurance like the contract read.'" Within days, Dick Moss, counsel for the MLBPA, told Kuhn to inform the 24 MLB teams that when Hunter's contract expired, he was to be a free agent. For one final occasion, Finley tried to play for time, lining up a series of reasons why he hadn't defaulted on the contract — and that even if he had, he still had time to make good.

With that final gambit, the MLBPA requested the arbitration case Miller had been waiting for since taking over the union. The arbitrator chosen was a man named Peter Seitz, a veteran labor lawyer who had served on the National Wage Stabilization Board and had been director of industrial relations for the Defense Department. On November 26, 1974, he heard arguments from the two sides. "We saw this as an open-and-shut case, a real winner," Miller said later. "The contract language wasn't even nego- tiated language. It was there before me, put in there by the owners and their lawyers. Any ambiguity would go against you in that circumstance. This language was clear-cut: 'If there is a violation of the contract, the player has the right to send notice to the club, calling attention to the viola- tion.' Hunter did that. The club has 10 days to correct the violation. If the club does that, that's the end of it. The Oakland club did not correct the violation."

The MLB lawyers ran through a series of Finley alibis. "My confidence grew as the hearing developed," Miller said. "Seitz was a perceptive, acute man. It was clear he was not buying Finley's story when Charlie said he knew nothing about this and claimed he did not understand the deferred payments." Seitz ruled on December 16, 1974, that Finley had violated Hunter's contract, with the remedy being that Catfish was now a free agent. Seitz took care to reject every one of Finley's lame reasons for not fulfilling the contract. He pointed out how many opportunities Finley had been given by Cherry to make good. Had he done so, baseball would have been spared this moment.

But Finley trusted that MLB could bail him out, as it had always rescued its blundering executives. This time it was not to be. Catfish Hunter, arguably the top starting pitcher in baseball, was about to become the first free agent of any consequence to experience the free market. A dazed Hunter himself didn't know what to think. "I hung up the phone, turned to my wife and said, 'We don't belong to anybody.' I was scared. I didn't have a job. I didn't realize the implications."

The implications made themselves obvious within 48 hours of the decision. Some speculated that only a few clubs might make a run at Hunter, or that owners might collude to thwart his attempt to get what he wanted; the price was expected to be about $250,000 to $350,000 per year. But in December 1974, almost every Major League club kicked the tires on Hunter. More than a dozen flew into his tiny town in North Carolina to make their pitch in person. All of Miller's dreams for his members' financial futures were realized as clubs fell all over each other trying to get Hunter.

On December 31, barely more than two weeks after Seitz granted him his freedom, Hunter signed a five-year deal worth a total of $3.5 million with the New York Yankees. George Steinbrenner, the ambitious Yankees owner, threw in a $1 million signing bonus as well. Marvin Miller was vindicated. Baseball executives' worst fears about free agency were realized. They knew they could never control themselves in an open market for talent.

It was about to get worse for owners, however. Hunter had earned his free agency through the pigheaded stupidity of Finley on a contract clause, not the end of the reserve clause. The finishing blow to the reserve clause would be another ruling by Seitz in 1976. There were more players than just Ted Simmons trying to test the one-year exemption to the reserve clause. But all the players eventually signed contracts before they'd completed a full year under the terms of their previous contract. Sparky Lyle of the Yankees and Bobby Tolan of the Padres both signed to healthy raises in the final week of the 1974 season after owners grew nervous about testing the reserve clause in court.

The following season, however, there were two players determined to play out their one-year options. Andy Messersmith, a star pitcher for the Los Angeles Dodgers, and veteran Dave McNally became the guinea pigs for the MLB Players Association to put the case before Seitz, the independent arbitrator. Messersmith acted after the Dodgers refused to give him a no-trade clause in his new contract. McNally, who'd been a perennial 20-game winner for the Orioles, had been traded to Montreal and was not happy with the contract offer, leaving the team after only nine games pitched. Although McNally retired halfway through the season, he was eligible to grieve his status. And since he was retired, he had no fear of repercussions from MLB teams.

How worried was MLB about its prospects, arguing before Seitz? Montreal Expos president John McHale flew to McNally's hometown of Billings, Montana, that

November to offer McNally $125,000 to play the 1976 season and a $25,000 bonus just for showing up at Expos training camp the following spring. McNally left the bonus on the table, turned down the contract and threw in his lot with Messersmith. The fight was on. First, the owners' representatives went to federal court to argue that Seitz didn't have the jurisdiction to hear the case. They claimed the union had promised not to challenge the reserve clause for the three years of the CBA. The appeal was denied.

With that door closed to them, the owners then made a fatal mistake in advance of the hearing before the independent arbitrator. Under terms of the CBA, they could have fired Seitz after his Hunter decision. Inexplicably, after seeing Seitz in action, the owners let him hear the Messersmith/McNally case. When the grievance hearing opened, they argued that players were obliged under the CBA to sign the basic contract when they played — a contract that included the reserve clause. The union countered by arguing that the meaning of article 10A meant exactly what it said: a one-year option to the previous employer, then freedom.

Seitz decided on behalf of the players, and over 50 years of baseball's absolute control over the players disappeared with Seitz's signature. The owners finally fired Seitz and went to federal court again to have a judge overturn his binding decision on a collectively bargained issue. That was denied, as was an attempt to have the appeals court overturn Seitz's decision. Baseball was faced with its worst nightmare — an entire league of players playing out their contracts to achieve free agency.

In some respects, unlimited free agency was a night-mare for Miller, too. The wily Miller understood that too many free agents in the market would only depress salaries and benefits. He needed to thread the needle of allowing free agency in the next CBA without having too many of his members avail themselves of the freedom. So in the CBA negotiations of 1976, Miller bargained to allow players to play out their option after six years in the majors; they could demand a trade after five full seasons in MLB. Miller also knew that most players in their seventh year were coming off their peak performance years, making them exceedingly attractive in the moment. As owners would learn, they were going to pay premium prices for fading stars in free agency.

Dazed owners gladly accepted the restrictions proposed by Miller, forgetting that limiting the number of prime players available was sure to cost them dearly. And it did. Messersmith signed a three-year deal worth $1 million with Atlanta (McNally stayed retired in Billings). Superstars cashed in. Reggie Jackson left the Oakland A's to sign with the Yankees for a then-record $3.5 million over five years.

The compromise of 1976 soon soured the owners on free agency and on each other. Teams were bidding wildly to pick up free agents, driving prices for talent ever higher. Mediocre players were cashing in. The bottom line for owners was being strained. They declared war on Miller and the Players Association. In the years leading up to 1995, owners and players would engage in three bloody labor stoppages over the issue of capping salaries for players. The final 1994 strike by players cost that year's

World Series and did immeasurable damage to the image of Major League Baseball and its players.

From the ashes of that disaster came baseball's luxury-tax system, which caps team payrolls but allows teams to exceed the cap if they pay a luxury tax on every dollar by which they exceed the cap, penalizing the team a percentage of the amount by which they exceed the soft cap. The percentage increases as the number of consecutive years a team exceeds the cap grows, resetting only when a team gets its payroll back under the cap. With some alterations, that is the system in effect in baseball today. It puts MLB alone in the company of North American pro team sports that otherwise all use a salary-cap system to control costs. How that has affected the quality of play will be examined in the upcoming pages.

1.4 BOBBY HULL

As the Supreme Court was considering *Flood v. Kuhn* in the summer of 1972, a team of elite Canadian hockey players was gathering to face the Soviet Union in an epic eight-game series. It was the first chance for Canada's best professionals to play the Soviets, who dominated so-called amateur hockey at the time, winning the past three Winter Olympic gold medals. Canadians were looking to reestablish their credentials as the dominant hockey nation in the world.

The Canadian team featured stars such as Phil and Tony Esposito, Wayne Cashman, Yvan Cournoyer, Ken Dryden and Brad Park. Bobby Orr, the greatest player in the National Hockey League at the time, was not able to play due to a knee problem, one that would end his career four years later. Another prominent name was missing as well. The man who had electrified scoring in the NHL by breaking Rocket Richard's single-season goal-scoring mark. The Golden Jet, Bobby Hull, was not a part of the squad. Hull was not injured, however. Hull was being excluded from this prestigious team because he'd offended the NHL, whose permission was needed to approve the Soviet–Canada series.

Hull's offense was to have signed a contract for his true market value in another league after years of being underpaid as the superstar of the Chicago Black Hawks. He'd led the NHL in goal scoring seven times during the 1960s. By his final NHL season in Chicago, he had broken the 50-goal per season barrier five times. Hull ended his 14-year NHL career in 1972 with 605 goals, 554 assists, 1,159 points, three Art Ross Trophies, two Hart Memorial Trophies, a Lady Byng Memorial Trophy and a Stanley Cup championship in 1961.

Bobby Hull and Gordie Howe were the two stars who had helped build the NHL in the United States. Both had plenty of leverage and would have been snapped up in a second by any of the other NHL teams in a free-agent market. But with the NHL operating a reserve clause similar to the one Flood had rebelled against in MLB, they were unable to get anything like their market value.

NHL owners could simply roll over the one-year option on the player's contract, depriving him of the chance to negotiate with other teams or gain any leverage with his current team. With NHL president Clarence

Campbell as the arbiter of all contract disputes at the time, players knew they'd never get a fair shake. The fledgling NHL Players' Association, under the corrupt Alan Eagleson, showed no sign of upsetting the status quo.

Hull had long feuded with Chicago owners Jim Norris and Bill Wirtz over his compensation. In 1969, he'd skipped the first month of the regular season in protest of how the terms of his four-year contract were being applied. By the summer of 1972 he was making $90,000 a year on his expiring contract — generous by NHL standards but ridiculous compared to the value of Hull's brand to the NHL across North America.

Bob Verdi of the *Chicago Tribune* described Hull as "the star of stars, yet he can be one of the guys. He is constantly badgered for this or that, yet he always has time to oblige a youngster's autograph pad. While his famous slapshot is a terrifying 115 miles per hour blur, the man behind it can be almost gentle — an excellent conversationalist, a jokester, just a nice fellow who carries his fame as aptly as he jettisons the puck."

Hull was restless and feeling unappreciated. Fortunately for him, there was a group of people feeling similarly unappreciated by the NHL. Even though Canada was the home of hockey, the NHL had been very slow to recognize the Canadian market. With the cooperation of the Toronto Maple Leafs and Montreal Canadiens, it had ignored Vancouver in the 1967 expansion to 12 teams, as the Canadian teams were reluctant to share their national market and TV contract. While Vancouver got an NHL team in 1970, Edmonton, Calgary, Winnipeg, Quebec City and southern Ontario were all ignored as potential sites for a pro hockey team. Both fans and politicians were making ominous noises about boycotting the league or looking at its monopoly status in both Canada and the United States. Canadian prime minister Lester B. Pearson stated that "the NHL decision to expand only in the U.S. impinges on the sacred principles of all Canadians."

While the NHL stuck to its business model, American sports investors saw the success of upstart leagues such as the American Football League and the American Basketball Association at attracting network TV money. Maybe they, too, could grab a piece of the exploding communications market in the U.S. not yet satisfied by the NHL. Their plans made it into the media. As a preemptory move, the NHL had added new teams in Vancouver and Buffalo in 1970, and in Long Island and Atlanta in 1972. But there were still plenty of major metropolitan areas available in the U.S.

Enter sports entrepreneurs Gary Davidson and Dennis Murphy, the men who'd given the ABA its start a few years earlier, in 1967. Looking for fresh horizons, they fixed on the sport of hockey, then run as a fiefdom by a few powerful owners who wanted no competition within the NHL or outside it. Using the template that had worked in recruiting owners to the ABA, Davidson and Murphy hooked up with Canadian businessman Bill Hunter to assemble cities interested in hockey as members of the World Hockey Association.

One of the opportunities Hunter had identified was the supply of Canadian cities that wanted to go big time. A Canadian division of untapped markets was a natural fit. They also saw that the NHL's average salary under its skinflint owners was $25,000 a year — the lowest of the four major team sports at the time. The WHA owners were willing to give the NHL a salary war, bidding up the price of hockey talent. This gave them instant credibility in recruiting even the best players in the NHL and eventually Europe.

Finally, the WHA would eschew the reserve clause. Anticipating legal developments on the horizon that would create antitrust nightmares for the establishment leagues, Davidson, Murphy and Hunter settled on a less restrictive contract formula. While not the direct child of *Flood v. Kuhn,* the WHA's abandonment of the reserve clause would have pleased Flood and Marvin Miller, who were trying to show baseball players the advantages of using labor stoppages to get a free market.

Looking over the NHL playing roster, there were a few names that could send a message to the established league that they were in for a fight. Orr was too closely tied to NHL Players' Association director Alan Eagleson, who was in the pocket of the NHL owners. Phil Esposito was not inclined to make waves. But there were a few players whose contracts were expiring who might be just what Davidson, Murphy and Hunter were looking for.

At the top the list was Hull, the name most Americans had associated with hockey for the past decade. Hull's salary problems with Chicago were well-known. He'd recently boycotted three days of training camp after the Hawks owners wouldn't let his children skate on the arena ice. He was a man of strong opinions and unlikely to shrink from a challenge after so many disappointments with Chicago's owners. But it would take a dramatic offer to shake the Golden Jet from Chicago, where he was a sports icon on a par with Ernie Banks and Dick Butkus.

It was Ben Hatskin, the owner of the Winnipeg Jets, who agreed to pay Hull a million dollars to have him in the WHA. Hatskin was one of several Canadian businessmen rebuffed by the NHL for expansion in 1967. He wanted pro hockey in his hometown and told his family he was going to lure Hull to the Manitoba capital. Hatskin was able to afford the yearly $250,000 salary for Hull, but it was going to take a dramatic bonus to seal the deal — a bonus he couldn't afford.

In the spring of 1972, Hull's lawyer was approached by Hatskin asking what it would take to bring him to a new league and a new city. Hull told his lawyer to tell the Jets it would take a million dollars. Hull contends the remark was made in jest to get Winnipeg to stop bugging him. If it was a joke, Hatskin wasn't laughing. He appealed to the other WHA owners to help him pony up the money. At first, a number of them balked at the idea. They didn't want to pay to see Hull come into their arena and beat the home team. The owners and their fans wanted to win, too.

But Hatskin made the plea to his fellow owners that if they couldn't sign Hull, there wouldn't be any fans coming into their arenas, win or lose. Hull would be a tide that raised all their boats. Eventually they saw the wisdom of Hatskin's suggestion, and the million-dollar bonus was made available to lure Hull. Meanwhile, Hull was having his usual friction with the Hawks over his salary. When Hatskin made good on Hull's facetious remark about the million dollars, Hull was at least willing to consider it.

Hull was impressed by the money offer, but he was

also impressed by the sincerity of Hatskin — a far cry from the take-it-or-leave-it attitude he had experienced from the Hawks owners. Loyalty to the Golden Jet was in short supply in Chicago. Still, he went back to the Hawks with the Jets' offer, asking them what they were going to do. Chicago owner Bill Wirtz proclaimed the whole thing a publicity stunt meant to force the Hawks' hand. He wasn't going to be railroaded by some upstart league and a hockey player, even if that player was Bobby Hull.

The Black Hawks' intransigence was the last straw. Hull cast his lot with the Jets and the WHA. Ben Hatskin had won his bet. Said former Jets goaltender Joe Daley, "Thank God that Benny was involved. To think that he had the mindset to say 'I'm going to go after Bobby Hull and I'm gonna get him,' and he actually did."

To say it was a seismic shock to a team and league that had always gotten its way is an understatement. The Black Hawks, stung by Hull's display of independence, publicly ripped him for his lack of loyalty to the fans and city of Chicago. They predicted he'd be back on his knees when the WHA folded within six months. They threatened to go to court to keep Hull in Chicago (until they were told that invoking the reserve clause in a court was not the wisest move the Hawks could make on behalf of the NHL).

The league piled on, declaring that Hull couldn't play for Team Canada against the Soviet Union (a move supported by Eagleson) in the 1972 Summit Series. They would rather see the Canadians lose to the Soviets than have Hull pollute their players with messages about the new league.

But the message was sent to the NHL that Hull's bold

move had changed its business. That summer, NHL stars J.C. Tremblay, Derek Sanderson, Bernie Parent, Gerry Cheevers and Ted Green signed big-money deals that dwarfed their NHL contracts. In all, 67 players jumped leagues to join Hull in the first year of the WHA. In subsequent years, the WHA lured players like Frank Mahovlich, Gordie Howe (and two of his sons), Paul Henderson, Marc Tardif and Réjean Houle. It also imported some of the top European players, with Ulf Nilsson and Anders Hedberg joining Hull on a line with the Jets — who won three WHA titles. The NHL and WHA soon ended up in court as the NHL attempted to restrict its players from jumping ship to the WHA.

Until it folded in 1979, the WHA was the best friend hockey players ever had, driving up salaries and benefits in both leagues. Some NHL teams, like Chicago, refused to recognize the change in the business and thereby lost stars such as Hull. Others, like the New York Rangers, paid the new rates to keep their stars from jumping. Sadly for players, the boon ended when the NHL and WHA merged in 1979, as the WHA could no longer afford to operate.

Players were given a chance to press the owners for concessions at the time of the merger, but NHLPA president Phil Esposito bought into the NHL's claims of financial distress. He declined to press for greater free agency or other benefits from the NHL. As a result, salaries were depressed again from 1980 to 1991 with the collusion of Eagleson at the NHLPA. Meaningful free agency would have to wait until Eagleson resigned in disgrace as NHLPA director in 1992.

Why is the Hull signing so important? Other leagues,

such as the AFL and the ABA, had also formed as challengers to their older competitors of the NFL and NBA. What made Hull-to-the-Jets significant was the message that one player could grant instant credibility to a league. The AFL formed in 1960 with a collection of ragtag players. There was no epic signing to frighten the NFL the way Hull's signing shocked the complacent NHL. Yes, the AFL added stars such as Joe Namath and Lance Alworth along the way. But as great as these players were, their brand couldn't match Hull's.

The ABA did manage a splashy signing in year one with the acquisition of Rick Barry, the star of the San Francisco Warriors. But under the NBA reserve clause, Barry still owed the Warriors a year on his contract — a condition upheld in court before *Flood v. Kuhn*. Barry was forced to sit out the entire 1967–68 season before he was free to play for the Oakland Oaks (owned by singer Pat Boone and coached by Barry's father-in-law, Bruce Hale).

But for owners in the 1970s, watching Hull's contract tower over the average salary of their leagues was intolerable. With courts and arbitrators getting closer to eliminating the reserve clause, something would be needed to prevent players like Hull from exercising their market value — and emboldening other leagues to compete with them.

1.5 MAGIC AND BIRD

As Major League Baseball players earned their freedom in the middle of the 1970s, players in the National Basketball Association had been struggling with their reserve clause since the inception of the league in 1946. For much of that time, their league was a far cry financially from baseball, the national pastime. Where Supreme Court justices swooned over the Lords of Baseball, few people had reverence for basketball's leaders. If you were serious about basketball, it was the college variety, not the NBA.

Conditions improved for the NBA somewhat in the 1960s as national television revenues became a possibility. A league that was a child of the radio era burst onto TV screens with the exploits of the great Boston Celtics, Los Angeles Lakers and Philadelphia 76ers of the decade. Pro basketball became the equal of the NCAA version. Its integrated lineups were also a symbol of the racial progress being made in the '60s.

Despite these improvements in the NBA's status, there simply wasn't a lot of money for a player to hit the big time by moving to another city. With no guaranteed contracts, only top stars like Bill Russell, Bob Cousy, Oscar Robertson and Wilt Chamberlain had even a shred of security in those years. "There was no pension plan, no per diem, no minimum wage, no health benefits and the average player salary was $8,000. It was not until 1964, when the NBA All-Star team threatened not to play in the first televised All-Star Game, that the players gained their first victory," says the NBPA website.

It took the players meeting with the powerful AFL-CIO union about organizing as a union for owners to finally take them seriously. There were other forces working on the NBA owners to update their business relationship with players. By the mid-'70s, the NBA was a besieged business. Oscar Robertson, then president of the NBPA, lent his name to a suit launched in 1970 by the players' union claiming antitrust violations against players. Legal costs were significant as the NBA sought to hold off the gains athletes were making in other sports. Added to its player issues, a long war with the upstart American Basketball Association (started in 1967) for prospects coming out of the NCAA had sent salaries soaring.

Unlike with baseball, this time it was the courts that set the athletes free. In 1971, the U.S. Supreme Court decision *Haywood v. National Basketball Association* ruled 7–2 against the NBA's requirement that a player wait four years after high school graduation before turning pro. That forced the NBA to allow players to enter the NBA Draft without completing college — provided they could show evidence of hardship to the NBA office.

In response, the ABA decided it would draft players after they completed high school as a matter of course. Using the change in rules, the Utah Stars of the ABA selected future superstar Moses Malone out of high school in the 1974 ABA Draft. Faced with seeing many of the top prospects snatched before they could even draft them, the NBA was forced to match in 1975, when two high school players, Darryl Dawkins and Bill Willoughby, used the league's financial hardship provision to start their professional careers early.

Meanwhile, the NBA's public image was a mess. Its TV partners were running its championship series games on a tape-delayed basis late at night. And the league was perceived, unfairly, as a black league with too many drug takers. Even with stars like Kareem Abdul-Jabbar, Julius Erving, George Gervin and Elvin Hayes, it was an uphill battle to win widespread support from advertisers and networks.

The NBA's first step to rebuilding its brand was to effect a merger with the ABA to end the bidding wars. Four teams from the ABA were eventually integrated into the league in the 1976 merger. Facing pressure from the U.S. Justice Department over its monopoly status after the ABA folded, the league was forced by the NBPA to eliminate the option clause that bound players to their clubs in perpetuity. The minimum salary jumped to $30,000 a year and health and dental benefits were added. In addition, the owners paid five hundred players a total of $4.3 million as a settlement and the union $1 million for legal fees, pending dismissal of the Oscar Robertson suit. It was a costly time to own an NBA team.

In the late 1970s, however, a glimmer of hope emerged that the NBA might be turning a corner financially. Adopting the ABA's three-point line proved a dynamic innovation in the way the game was played on the court. Then, in 1979, two young stars arrived to push the NBA into a new era. Earvin "Magic" Johnson and Larry Bird became the great rivals of the next decade. Johnson was the dynamic Michigan State star who could play guard or even center if needed for the L.A. Lakers. Bird was the gangly "Hick from French Lick," the hot-shooting geek on the Boston Celtics who played better as the games got closer. It was a narrative the NBA would ride for the next decade.

With the Magic & Bird Show — and the arrival of the league's new commissioner, David Stern, in 1984 — the league was poised to embark on a generation of prosperity and popularity on network TV and with sponsors. Stern would marry urban culture to the explosion in apparel sales to make the NBA a "must-buy" for advertisers. A young North Carolina product who arrived in Stern's first year was also helpful when he succeeded Bird and Johnson — a shooting guard named Michael Jordan.

To create a financial platform for this growth, however, the NBA felt it needed to get a handle on its player payroll in the early '80s. Owners were giving out large contracts to secondary players; teams were relocating to new cities even as the league expanded to 21 teams. NBA national TV revenues were far behind those of the NFL and MLB. Many teams were in trouble, making ends meet from local revenues. It was a recipe for disaster. Critically, the NBA players' union bought into the league's concept that the NBA needed a fundamental fix.

To bring financial stability to the sport, NBA commissioner Larry O'Brien and NBPA director Paul Silas engaged in negotiations in 1983 to create a restraint on team salaries to begin in 1983–84. Or, as it has become known, a salary cap. They settled on having 53 percent of designated league revenues — or $3.6 million per team — as the players' share. Teams would be forced to stay below this number. This was known as a hard cap — the first collectively bargained restraint on salaries in North American team sports.

Going into the season, five teams had payrolls over the $3.5 million cap. These teams faced a critical situation as the clock ticked down to the implementation of the cap: they might not have left enough money to sign their top stars heading into new negotiations. That was especially true of the Boston Celtics, who had their young star Bird coming up for a new deal before 1983–84. If the cap remained hard, they would have to cut several of the players who had won the 1981 NBA title and remained favorites for the 1983–84 title.

Bird was more than just a star in a league that was full of dynamic stars. He was a trash-talking white star in a league that was 80 percent black. More importantly, he was the yin to Magic Johnson's yang, the eastern star who would lead his Celtics against the Lakers and their western star in riveting NBA Finals three times over the decade. Their rivalry then carried over into commercials, the NBA Three-Point Contest and first-ballot competition for the Hall of Fame.

Bird also played for the prestige franchise of the NBA, the Celtics, winners of 11 of 13 NBA titles from 1957 to 1969. What was good for the Celtics was invariably good for the NBA. And what was good for the Celtics in 1983 was to keep Larry Bird and as many of the other championship players as possible. Boston knew that finding the money to pay Bird after the cap kicked in might cost them Kevin McHale, who was being sought-after by the New York Knicks.

Here is how the NBA's hard salary cap went soft. Franchises like Boston needed to be able to tell their fans they were keeping their favorite players that they'd drafted and developed. So after they'd crafted the hard cap, the owners and players agreed on something called the "qualifying veteran free agents" clause.

Bearing in mind the Celtics' dilemma, this clause almost immediately became known as the "Larry Bird exception." It allows teams to go over the salary cap to re-sign their own free agents "at an amount up to the (NBA) maximum salary." According to the NBA, to qualify as a Bird free agent, a player must have played three seasons without being waived or changing teams as a free agent. Teams could match any offer sheets given to the free-agent player by another team or simply sign their player a new contract using the financial advantage bestowed by the Bird rule.

Today, after some CBA tweaking, NBA free agents are limited to five-year contracts if they sign with another team. They can sign six-year contracts with their own team, however. Their own team can also give them larger yearly increases in salary than other teams can. In short, the Larry Bird rule is a great assistance to a team hoping to keep its roster together.

Ironically, the Larry Bird exception was not used to sign Bird himself that year. Just before the terms of the CBA kicked in, Bird signed a then-record seven-year contract worth $12.6 million, taking him off the market. So the Celtics then turned around and used the Larry Bird clause to sign forward Cedric "Cornbread" Maxwell. It also left them enough money to re-sign McHale. The Celtics did use the Bird exception on Bird himself when his seven-year deal expired.

Now the NBA cap is a soft cap with exceptions. Over the years, the NBA and its players underwent labor stoppages as the epic 1983 CBA was tinkered with. The mid-level agreement, the Derrick Rose rule and the designated-player exception now allow teams to operate more freely under a soft cap by exceeding their annual cap number. To cope with the salary-cap rules and stay in compliance, NBA teams began using executives with financial backgrounds to guide their franchises instead of old-fashioned basketball executives. And so the 1983 CBA changed not only how lineups were constructed but also how teams would organize their front offices in the decades to come.

None of the NFL, NHL or MLB had anything like the salary cap or the Bird exception in 1983 to assist them in controlling their player payrolls. But they would all soon come knocking on the doors of their players' unions, demanding that they, too, control finances by adopting a salary-cap rule. And just as certainly, the players' unions would push back, causing strikes and lockouts in all the sports over the subsequent decades. The significance of the NBA's adopting of the salary cap was the cooperation of a players' union in accepting a brake to forgive the owners' undisciplined spending. In addition to the arcane details of the NBA's cap, the acceptance by players was also duly noted by the rival leagues. The salary-cap dam had been breached. Public pressure could force the players to buckle. The repercussions would still be echoing 35 years later.

1.6 REGGIE WHITE

Reggie White was truly a mountain of a man. Named the "Minister of Defense" for his football skill and his religious faith, White came out of the University of Tennessee in 1984 to star in the USFL for two years and then in the NFL as a defensive tackle for 15 seasons. He twice won NFL Defensive Player of the Year. He was a 13-time Pro Bowl and 13-time All-Pro selection. White still ranks second all-time among career sack leaders with 198 (behind Bruce Smith). The six-foot-five, 300-pound product of Chattanooga was selected to the NFL 75th Anniversary All-Time Team and the NFL's 1980s and '90s All-Decade Teams.

But even as he terrorized NFL quarterbacks and offensive linemen — and was among the game's signature players — White was unhappy with his ability to determine his football destiny. Under the NFL standard contract, he had no choice but to play for the Philadelphia Eagles, the team that drafted him and maintained his rights in the NFL after the USFL folded. With his impressive resumé, White knew he could dictate his choices in a free market. But White felt that he and his fellow players were being illegally restrained from playing where they wanted and for how much money.

Like the NBA, NHL and MLB, the NFL had employed a reserve rule with rights to permanently renew expiring contracts. White's union, the NFL Players Association, had been trying for years to have the reserve rule tossed out. To avoid the scrutiny of the U.S. Justice Department, the NFL created the so-called "Rozelle Rule," named for the NFL commissioner who'd created it. Employed to give the appearance of free agency — and avoid antitrust scrutiny — the rule required a team signing a free agent to compensate that player's former team by means of players and/or draft selections.

Should these teams be unable to agree, Rozelle was to arbitrate the matter, fixing the compensation. Rozelle ruled just five times from a possible 176 cases in 12 years. But the dampening effect on clubs wishing to sign a free agent was clear. Without knowing which players or draft choices Rozelle might select as compensation, arbitration was too much of a gamble for most teams.

The Rozelle Rule was eventually declared a violation of antitrust laws in 1975 in the case *Mackey v. NFL* as it was imposed by the league, and not a product of "bona fide arm's-length bargaining over the Rozelle Rule . . . remain[ing] unchanged since it was unilaterally promulgated by the clubs in 1963." So the NFL tweaked the formula to create a similar compensation system, getting it agreed to in the next CBA to gain protection by U.S. labor law. Known as Plan B, this gave teams first right of refusal and tied compensation to draft picks awarded on the basis of salaries received by departing free agents. This system, too, proved an effective barrier to players' movement.

A frustrated NFLPA conducted two largely unsuccessful strikes in 1982 and 1987 to liberalize player movement. The 1982 strike was crushed, as the players revolted against their own union executive over its strategy. The only products of the strike for players in the new five-year agreement were severance packages to players upon retirement, an increase in salaries and postseason pay and bonuses based on the number of years of experience in the league.

Additionally, and often underestimated in its importance, the NFLPA was allowed to receive copies of all player contracts. With just one of five hundred eligible players receiving a free-agent offer in 1982, the farce of liberalized free agency became a rallying cry for players in the next CBA. Anticipating possible trouble with its antitrust status, the NFL allowed teams to protect 37 roster players from entering the free-agent market and stipulated that teams could retain their free agents by matching any offers or else receive compensation from a pool of players not on the protected lists.

When the five-year deal between NFL and NFLPA ended in 1987, the players again went on strike, this time under the leadership of former NFL star Gene Upshaw. Owners responded by suiting up scab teams of replacement players to replace the stars. Again, disharmony among the union membership resulted in a collapse of the strike. The defection of 87 players back to the league's replacement teams undermined the labor action. In particular, the defection of a number of the NFL's top stars — including Joe Montana, Lawrence Taylor, Tony Dorsett, Randy White, Danny White, Steve Largent, Ed "Too Tall" Jones and Mark Gastineau — made the strike unsustainable.

Players went back to work on October 15, 1987, joining some of the replacement players whom they had ostracized for months. One of the union diehards who reported that day was Reggie White, the ordained minister, still hoping to find some way to change the NFL's rules on player movement. The day White reported, the NFLPA filed an antitrust lawsuit — named *Powell v. NFL* after NFLPA President Marvin Powell — against the NFL in federal court in Minnesota. It challenged Plan B.

In 1989, Judge David Doty in Minneapolis agreed with players, saying that the owners were in violation of antitrust rules with Plan B and other restraints. The

NFLPA thought it had won the day, but that decision was reversed on appeal. The appellate judges contended that since the NFLPA was a certified union it could receive no remedies under the *Sherman Act*. Any changes would have to be collectively bargained. As the NFL refused to bargain away its first right of refusal and compensation system, the NFLPA seemed backed into a corner.

Desperate to get a win in court, the players decided to decertify their union to create a professional association. They would lose some of the protections of U.S. labor law, but they would now be able to use the *Sherman Act* to their benefit. The NFLPA launched the case known as *McNeil v. NFL* to claim damages from Plan B on behalf of eight players (Freeman McNeil of the Jets, Don Majkowski of the Packers, Tim McDonald of the Cardinals, Niko Noga of the Lions, Mark Collins and Lee Rouson of the Giants, Dave Richards from the Chargers and Frank Minnifield of the Browns). The NFL argued that the NFLPA was just a "union in hiding" and that it had only dropped its union status to get around the appellate court ruling that said it could not be protected by the *Sherman Act*.

The NFLPA gamble paid off. With its new decertified status, the NFL players' union finally won a decisive court victory in 1992 over the NFL on Plan B. While the decision only immediately affected the eight players named in the suit with just four receiving financial compensation, it created a framework that threatened the owners' hegemony over players.

Still, it remained only a symbolic victory. The league fought back on its desire to restrict players like Reggie White from finding an open market for their skills. There had been no new CBA since the 1982 agreement expired in 1987. To drain the NFLPA's bank account, the NFL had created a "Quarterback Club" marketing arm. The "Quarterback Club" featured 40 of the league's top QBs and some select others, who were handsomely compensated with bonuses and percentages of sales. The move prevented the NFLPA from using many of its top players for marketing purposes, denying significant marketing revenues to the rest of the players and the NFLPA. The NFLPA responded in kind with Players Inc. in 1994, evening the playing field a little.

Even as they cheered the Plan B decision, the players knew that they needed to move quickly. That did not mean collective bargaining with the NFL, which still believed it could break the union at will. One more time, the NFLPA went to the courts. This time it was a 1992 class-action suit claiming that the NFL had restricted the rights of one of its most decorated stars: Reggie White. By this point, White was nearing the end of his contract with the Eagles. Under the current regime, he had few options. Getting the courts to force the NFL to open up free agency would be a boon to him. The complaint sought "antitrust injunctive relief and damages stemming from various league rules, including the mandatory right of first refusal system, the standard NFL contract and the college draft." Most worrying for the NFL, players would be awarded treble damages if they won.

By this point, the public was largely numb to the legal mumbo jumbo coming out of its favorite Sunday afternoon diversion. All it wanted was anything that could keep the two sides from another labor stoppage. In *White v. NFL*, Judge David Doty was again hearing the facts of the case. He felt much the same as the fans did. Both sides still had compelling arguments as to why they should prevail. The NFLPA was running short on money, and the NFL had not done well in court on the last few lawsuits. After decades of battling in and out of court, it was time to reach a negotiated settlement Doty told them: get one done or risk my decision being an unpleasant surprise.

White's lawsuit had broken the logjam. By early 1993, the NFLPA had recertified as a union so that it might bargain on behalf of the players. With the hammer of *White v. NFL* still in its pocket, the union had leverage for a change. While new NFL commissioner Paul Tagliabue had members who wanted to keep the court fights going until the union was broke, he also knew that developments in other sports were showing that the way forward lay in collective bargaining not antitrust lawsuits. Cutting a good deal at the bargaining table would be cost-effective, and with divisions still existing in the NFLPA, there was no guarantee that the league couldn't still get much of what it wanted in the new CBA.

The result of intensive negotiations in the spring of 1993, the new CBA finally gave NFL players some things they'd desired for years. First, they achieved free agency without compensation to the teams losing a player. Players would have to last four seasons to gain the right to bargain freely. The NFL's version of the salary cap also allowed for a "franchise player" tag. A veteran player getting free agency could be retained by his team under the franchise tag for a one-year salary equal to the average salary at his position across the league.

Players were also given a guaranteed 51 percent of NFL revenues, to be divided among the teams under a hard salary cap. No Larry Bird exceptions. No soft-cap exceptions. No mid-level exceptions. Live with it.

The owners made out just fine in the new deal, too. They had avoided guaranteed contracts, something both the NBA and NHL allowed. Players could be cut at any time. Owners determined the league's revenues, which meant they could slow the growth in team payrolls. Pension and post-career health benefits were also going to be depressed under this system.

It would soon be seen that the NFL owners had carved out the most generous salary-cap provisions in pro team sports — if you were an owner, that is. They continue to exercise that control almost undiminished to this day. The NFL is well-known for its non-guaranteed contracts. Under the "Physical Condition" clause, the team can cut a player if the player "fails to establish or maintain his excellent physical condition to the satisfaction of the Club physician . . ." Meanwhile, under the "Skill, Performance, and Conduct" clause, "If at any time, in the sole judgment of Club, Player's skill or performance has been unsatisfactory as compared with that of other players competing for positions on Club's roster, or if Player has engaged in personal conduct reasonably judged by a Club to adversely affect or reflect on Club, then Club may terminate this contract." In layman's terms, if an NFL team finds that it has a better player waiting in the wings, it can cut the current player. Or if an NFL team finds that a player has behaved badly — in its opinion —— then it can cut the player.

As for Reggie White, he became one of the first to benefit from the freedom to bargain he'd desired for so long. White signed as a free agent with the Green Bay Packers, where he continued his illustrious career — putting up another 68.5 sacks over six seasons to become the Packers' all-time leader in that category (two Packers have since eclipsed his record). He also helped the Packers win Super Bowl XXXI with a game-ending sack. He retired for one season then came back in 2000 to put up another 5.5 sacks for the Carolina Panthers.

White tragically died of heart disease at the age of 41, but his legacy as a player was intact, as was his legacy in gaining some measure of freedom for his teammates and the opponents he'd terrorized for years.

1.7 WAYNE GRETZKY

While Reggie White had been a determined warrior for NFL players' rights, NHL superstar Wayne Gretzky was a reluctant champion in helping NHL players catch up with their colleagues in other sports. In the summer of 1988, while White was perhaps the greatest defensive lineman in NFL history, Gretzky was the greatest offensive player ever in the NHL. He had already amassed many records that will never be matched, such as scoring 92 goals in a single season (1981–82), 163 assists in a season (1985–86) and more than two hundred points in a season three years in a row (no one else has ever scored more than two hundred once). All of this on the way to ten Art Ross Trophies as the NHL's top point scorer, nine Hart Trophies as the

NHL's MVP and 2,857 points over his career. These are but a few of the 61 records he holds or shares.

His Edmonton Oilers had won their fourth Stanley Cup in five years in the spring of 1988, led by their dynamic captain. Gretzky had also gotten married that summer to Hollywood actress Janet Jones. He was a national hero for having led Canada to victory in the Canada Cup over the USSR the previous year. But while his athletic exploits were unlimited, the financial landscape for players like him was harsh in the unforgiving NHL economy. After the halcyon days of Bobby Hull and the World Hockey Association — when players saw their salaries and leverage soar — Gretzky and his colleagues faced a far more restricted market for their services in 1988. The NHL he dominated was still a cozy cabal of a few owners, president John Ziegler and their house union, the NHLPA, led by Alan Eagleson. Meaningful free agency didn't exist, players had no independent arbitration (unlike MLB players) and there was no salary disclosure among players. On top of that, the pensions of retired players were at poverty level.

In this daunting financial environment, Gretzky had become a problem for the small-market Oilers; he was becoming too expensive an asset. Even though he was making a pittance next to the superstars in the other sports, his salary was still a burden for Edmonton owner Peter Pocklington — and it would only go higher. Pocklington had been having financial problems in his other businesses, putting pressure on him to hold the line on the Oilers payroll. While the notion of free agency for a player like Gretzky was still foreign to the NHL, Pocklington under-stood that his greatest asset was going to cost more — lots more — in the future. He was starting to heed advice that the 27-year-old Gretzky was going to depreciate in market value even as he commanded more salary.

In the summer of 1988, Pocklington reluctantly conceded that he needed to cash in his asset at its highest value. As the Oilers made their run to the 1988 Stanley Cup, he directed his general manager, Glen Sather, to find out what Gretzky might fetch in the trade market — even as he denied that Gretzky was in play, Sather canvassed the return for trading the greatest scoring machine the NHL had ever seen. Vancouver was interested. So were the New York Rangers and Detroit Red Wings. But there was also a mystery shopper involved.

While the NHL was still being run by a small group of established owners, a new wind was blowing in southern California. An ebullient coin dealer named Bruce McNall had purchased the Los Angeles Kings, and he was looking to make news in Hollywood. The Kings had always been underachievers, considering the size of their market — the second-largest media market in North America. The Kings had never won a semifinal series, let alone a Stanley Cup, since coming into the league in 1967 (although they did defeat Gretzky's Oilers three games to two in the 1982 playoffs — a series that included the "Miracle on Manchester," in which the Kings came back from a 5–0 deficit in Game 3 to win 6–5 in overtime). There was a sense that hockey would never work in the bright sunshine of Hollywood. The original Kings owner, Canadian Jack Kent Cooke, had thought he could count on expat Canadians filling his building. As a rueful Cooke later explained, "I found out why they left Canada. They hate hockey."

McNall understood that, with all the other distractions in L.A., winning was everything. Even then, winning might not be enough. To get the beautiful people from the entertainment industry to visit a hockey rink, you needed star power. No one, believed McNall, said star power in the NHL quite like Gretzky. These were all foreign concepts in the NHL, where players were disposable and the crest on the jersey was the only brand that mattered. The culture was deference and doing things the way they had always been done, which was "the right way." People who hung around hockey long enough called it the Game.

One of the people most deferential to the Game was Gretzky himself. Seemingly raised from birth to be a superstar, he embodied the humility gene found in Canadian stars such as Gordie Howe, Jean Béliveau and Bobby Orr. He referred to people as "Mr. Howe" or "Mr. Ziegler." His unadorned joy at playing hockey spoke of an uncomplicated loyalty to the myth of hockey as a pure ritual. While there had been attempts to reform the NHL Players' Association, the insurgents could never get Gretzky to support them. He spoke of not wanting to hurt the Game.

So you can imagine the reaction of Gretzky when the Oilers informed him that the most famous person in the history of Edmonton — perhaps the most famous person in Canada — was going to be traded (some might say sold) to the uninspiring Los Angeles Kings. On August 9, 1988, 12 weeks after the Oilers closed out a four-game sweep of the Boston Bruins in the Stanley Cup Finals, the news broke. The press conference to announce the sale was a wake, with a weeping Gretzky trying to find the words to describe his distress at seeing his loyalty to the Oilers tossed in the rubbish heap.

Sather looked like a man forced to sell his reputation at five cents on the dollar. Pocklington, too, was funereal as the weight of his enormous gamble settled on his shoulders, his name forever after to be associated with treachery. "My mistake was not going over to him and putting my arm around him and saying 'Wayne, it's OK, pal. If you want to call it off, let's do it,'" Pocklington said later. "That's what I should have done."

Pocklington got a much-needed $15 million for Gretzky, plus a handful of players (who'd all be gone within five years) and some draft picks (none of whom panned out for the Oilers). Going to the Kings with Gretzky were tough guy Marty McSorley and forward Mike Krushelnyski. The city of Edmonton, meanwhile, lost its innocence dealing with the new ways of pro sports.

The scene later the same day at the Sheraton Park Plaza in Hollywood was far different than the sepulchral scene in Edmonton. McNall had pulled out all the stops to let Los Angeles know that he was a player. "When I bought the team, [co-owner Jerry Buss] told me, 'I've been trying to talk to Peter Pocklington about Gretzky.' We all kind of laughed. But the fact that he brought up the subject gave me a sense that I could actually make that call," McNall told nhl.com years later.

The room had all the elements that make Hollywood what it is. There was a suntanned Gretzky and his actress wife, Janet. There was his family. There were new silver-and-black uniforms for the Kings. The media mob assembled looked like an NFL, MLB or NBA presser in L.A., not a typical NHL press availability. "There were about 12 television stations there, and I don't know how many photographers. It was obviously the biggest press conference the Kings ever had," longtime Kings broadcaster Bob Miller told nhl.com. "The sound of the cameras going off, my wife said it sounded like machine gun fire."

Having picked up Gretzky the way he picked up rare coins, McNall set about trying to put a value on his new player. Despite being the star of stars in the NHL, Gretzky was making less than a million dollars a year. To NHL players, a million dollars per year was serious money. But it would not do for McNall to have his precious asset priced like a buffalo nickel.

Gretzky and his agent, Mike Barnett, sat down to talk contract with McNall in the days after his arrival in SoCal. After the usual pleasantries, McNall got to the point. He wanted to pay Gretzky $3 million a year to be the captain of the Kings. According to Barnett, Gretzky demurred. He'd always been told there was just so much money for an NHL payroll, and if one player got too much there'd be none left for the others. Gretzky told McNall that he was concerned if he made that much, there might not be enough to make a winning team. Barnett said he almost kicked Gretzky under the table.

McNall, amused that Gretzky bought into the NHL owners' claims of hardship, reassured Gretzky that there would be money for players where front-row seats sold for $250 a pop (at a time when good seats in Edmonton might be $50). With no salary cap in the NHL, McNall could spend whatever he desired when the money from having Gretzky aboard rolled in. And so it was that the glass ceiling in the NHL was shattered when No. 99 got $2.5 million a year for seven years.

The numbers stunned the hockey world. What had McNall done, asked his fellow owners. Most toxic for the NHL owners was the public knowledge of Gretzky's contract. Until now, players almost never told each other, not even their roommates, what they made. NHLPA executive director Alan Eagleson rewarded his owner buddies by convincing players that salary disclosure would produce animosity among players. But now everyone knew what the league's bell cow was making. Mario Lemieux, who'd just won the Hart and Art Ross Trophies, could be expected to line up for a bump in his salary. Steve Yzerman, Ray Bourque, Patrick Roy and Paul Coffey would also want their cake.

To get the other trappings of a real union, however, players would need to divest themselves of NHLPA czar Alan Eagleson and establish a real bargaining position, not the sham negotiations that had characterized previous CBAs. Eagleson himself was not going to go willingly. It was at this point that the U.S. Department of Justice intervened. A crusading Boston-area journalist, Russ Conway, in concert with former NHLer Carl Brewer, had been exposing the fraudulent double-dealing done by Eagleson as head of the players' association. Along with CBC Toronto, they published a series of devastating reports on how the NHLPA was a house union, with the league allowing Eagleson to conduct international hockey in exchange for going easy in collective bargaining. In addition, it was revealed how Eagleson enriched himself from his position. Eagleson eventually pled guilty to fraud charges in the U.S. and Canada in 1998, serving four months in jail — and had his membership in the Order of Canada revoked, becoming the first person to be removed from the prestigious order since its creation in 1967.

In short order, the FBI raided league and union offices in search of documents. Eagleson was forced into retirement at the end of 1991, replaced by former agent Bob Goodenow. Goodenow's first order of business was to lead the players on a brief strike at the end of the 1991–92 season, just before the playoffs. Armed with knowledge of the reluctant Gretzky's contract and the pittance stars like Howe, Hull and Béliveau were making in their pensions, Goodenow was able to create the sort of union culture that Marvin Miller had produced among baseball players in the mid-1960s. While the players made only a few modest gains with the strike, they had set the stage for an escalation of salaries and benefits that would see them make as much as $10 million a year within a decade.

Led by Chicago owner Bill Wirtz, the league fought back to restore its whip hand over players. First it hired hard-line NBA executive Gary Bettman to become the NHL's first commissioner, with a mandate to get a salary cap. The NHL locked out its players three times — for half a season in the 1994–95 season, for a full season in 2004–05 and again for half a season in 2011–12 — in an attempt to moderate salaries. Players won the right to free agency for veteran players without a salary cap in the 1994–95 lockout. They caved on a salary cap in 2004–05 but won 57 percent of league revenues and more liberalized free agency starting as early as year five for a player, which cost Goodenow his job. In 2012–13 it was mostly givebacks by players, but they maintained liberal free agency, guaranteed contracts and a $60 million salary cap.

In truth, there was enough money in the business that CBA negotiations became a case of millionaires versus billionaires. That was a far cry from the day Gretzky was told he was being traded to Los Angeles. But the Reluctant One had also proved to be the Great One in pushing players to greater compensation and freedom.

1.8 SHAQUILLE O'NEAL

Through his trade to Los Angeles, Wayne Gretzky had cast a long shadow on his sport. The Great One left L.A. via trade to an ignominious stint in St. Louis in February 1996. The Great One was not the only one to depart L.A. The year before, both NFL teams, the Rams and Raiders, moved to St. Louis and Oakland, respectively. It looked like L.A. was no longer a sports town. But only a few months later, L.A. snagged its next big star — and its largest star. While No. 99's shadow was a metaphorical one, Shaquille O'Neal — everyone calls him Shaq — cast a literal shadow as big as a house. At seven-foot-one and 325 pounds in his NBA prime, Shaq was a condominium, not a shack, on the court. The heaviest man ever to lace up sneakers in the association until then, he was still agile and could move with some grace for a man his size. As shown by his career 58.2 percent shooting percentage — much of it accomplished in the paint — he also possessed unstoppable power when motivated to go to the hoop.

He'd been a prodigy in high school in San Antonio,

Texas, leading his team to a 68–1 record during his two years on the varsity. Recruited by every major program, he settled on Louisiana State University, just across the border from his Texas home. He'd met Dale Brown, the Tigers coach, while O'Neal's stepfather was stationed in Europe with the U.S. Army. At the time, NBA rules said he could enter the league if he could prove hardship. Instead he opted for two years in Baton Rouge. Once again, he was the dominant player, receiving the award as NCAA men's basketball Player of the Year in 1991.

The Orlando Magic had been perennial losers since beginning play in 1989. To say that they saw Shaq as the answer to their prayers understates central Florida's excitement to have this once-in-a-generation player arrive in the Theme Park Capital of the World. When O'Neal declared for the 1992 draft, it was a no-brainer for the Magic to select him.

As Shaq entered the NBA, he was considered the natural successor to NBA star-of-stars Michael Jordan of the Chicago Bulls and, before him, Magic Johnson and Larry Bird. It was Jordan who had realized the marketing dreams of NBA commissioner David Stern, taking the league from the bruising Bad Boys image of the two-time champion Detroit Pistons to a dynamic entertainment vehicle for skilled players such as Jordan.

Realizing that a synthesis of sports, pop culture and apparel sales could make the NBA rich, Stern oversaw the signing of Jordan to an enormous shoe contract with Portland-based sports apparel manufacturer Nike. In return for the Nike money, Stern made sure that the game graduated from its nasty under-the-rim violence to a wide-open spectacle highlighted by the airborne Jordan (whose "Jumpman" silhouette became the logo for Nike's Air Jordan shoes) flying over the rest of the league to the adulation of fans. That this happened in the third-largest media market in the U.S. was gravy.

With the allowance of the referees, Jordan was given the room to drive, slam and shoot. Fans couldn't get enough of him and his Bulls, who succeeded the Pistons and won six NBA titles in eight years under Phil Jackson's triangle offense. Fans also couldn't buy enough of Jordan's licensed merchandise, either. And they proved unable to resist Jordan's forays into pop culture via movies such as *Space Jam* and an appearance alongside Michael Jackson in Jackson's "Jam" music video. He was everywhere in the media, on multiple platforms.

The league boasted other dazzling performers, but O'Neal was considered the anointed one to take the torch from Jordan and spin off his exploits into a one-man entertainment industry. And not only with running shoes. O'Neal would make forays into movies, such as *Kazaam*, and music, even as he played in the NBA. TV couldn't get enough of him, and the NBA prospered at the same time. With all the money washing through the NBA, the sky was the limit for Shaq.

To many NBA owners, the salary sky was too high by the time Shaq brought his size-22 sneakers to the hardwood of the NBA. While the NBA had been the first league to agree to a salary cap with the CBA signed in 1983, the mood between owners and players was anything but cordial in the years after the signing. With another troublesome negotiation coming up in 1988, players saw that restrictions in the previous CBA concerning the salary cap and the college draft (among other things) were still affecting their free movement.

When owners showed little willingness to fine-tune the landmark 1983 deal, NBA players sought redress in the courts once again in 1987, this time with the *Junior Bridgeman v. NBA* suit, named for the president of the NBPA at the time. After the players received a favorable preliminary ruling, the owners opted to settle on a new six-year collective bargaining agreement. It called for the elimination of the right of first refusal after a player completed his second contract, unrestricted free agency for veteran players and the reduction of the NBA draft from three rounds to two by 1989.

Basketball fans hoped that this would eliminate the threat of further labor disruptions. But once again, the good feelings dissipated quickly. Bad blood between the sides simmered into 1991. By that point, the NBPA was complaining that the league was fudging its revenue numbers to create the illusion that it was making less money. With player salaries predicated on accurate numbers from the league (players were due 50 percent of revenues under the cap), this was a red flag to the NBPA. When it did not get the disclosures it sought, the players' union took the issue to arbitration. While some owners vowed to fight the case, the rest of the owners were not happy about having more drawn-out litigation on the horizon. So the NBA again reached a settlement with the NBPA, valued at $62 million in gains for the players.

O'Neal, meanwhile, had blossomed in Orlando, winning the 1993 Rookie of the Year award and leading the

Magic to the NBA Finals in 1995, where they lost to the Hakeem Olajuwon–led Houston Rockets. That 1994–95 season, Shaq led the NBA in scoring with a 29.3-point average, while finishing second in MVP voting to David Robinson of San Antonio. He had become everything that had been predicted for him. Teamed with the dynamic Penny Hardaway, he was a god in Orlando and already a fixture in league marketing. His 1993 debut rap album, *Shaq Diesel*, received platinum certification. He'd appeared in the 1994 film *Blue Chips*. In short, O'Neal was the very model of the modern superstar, earning buckets of money away from the court as well as on it.

After the excitement of the finals appearance in the spring of 1995, the next season, 1995–96, was a sour one for O'Neal. While his entertainment career grew, he was injured a great deal that season as he headed for free agency. Plus there was labor strife in the league. Owners had locked out the players right after the Magic were eliminated by the Rockets. The lockout had little effect on the regular season, as the sides settled quickly.

The NBA won a rookie wage scale, the allowable percentage increase in multi-year contracts was reduced from 30 percent to 20 percent and the length of a contract was restricted. For their part, players retained the Larry Bird exception (for retaining players in their current city at a higher pay grade). They also eliminated restricted free agency, with unrestricted free agency granted to all players after their contract expired — key for Shaq, whose own contract was expiring at the end of the 1996 playoffs.

The Magic, desperate to keep O'Neal, offered him

$115 million over seven seasons, but Shaq was not biting. Polls in the Orlando papers during 1996 said that an injury-plagued O'Neal wasn't worth the money and that he was undermining the authority of Magic head coach Brian Hill. A local writer suggested he was not a good role model for not marrying his girlfriend once they had their first child. When an out-of-retirement Jordan and the Bulls eliminated the Magic in the Eastern Conference Finals in 1996, the die was cast. Shaq was moving on, and there wasn't much the Magic could do about it.

There had never been as big a free agent, either in size or significance. On a basketball level, it was clear that any team adding Shaq was going to be an instant contender to win the NBA title. It seemed as if Hollywood or New York were the only places big enough to satisfy his basketball and entertainment ambitions. For a league that had just expanded into Canada in 1995 with the Toronto Raptors and Vancouver Grizzlies, the idea that small markets could not hold on to the stars they developed was poison to the equity of those new investors. Who would join a league with no chance of nurturing the players who could bring a championship?

To prove the point, O'Neal signed with the legendary Lakers while he was playing for the U.S. at the 1996 Olympics. The cost: $122 million over seven years. O'Neal was at pains to say that it was not a money decision: "I'm tired of hearing about money, money, money, money, money," he told reporters. "I just want to play the game, drink Pepsi, wear Reebok." Shaq was already making $17 million from his two sponsors by the time he was 23. Plus he wanted to make movies, cut records, design running-shoe lines, create video games, work as a TV analyst and generally do whatever he wanted to.

O'Neal wasn't the only NBA player making a lot of money — which was too much money for owners' liking. Pushed by O'Neal's record-setting contract, the price of hoop dreams was growing rapidly. By the 1997–98 season, the approximately 400 NBA players were collectively earning $1 billion in salaries and benefits. The owners claimed that player salaries were claiming 57 percent of revenues, whereas the figure had been closer to 43 percent in the prior CBA. They felt that the salary cap still had too many provisions to allow teams to pay players like Shaq exorbitant (to their mind) salaries and still maintain competitive balance.

If you're feeling bad for owners, keep in mind comedian Chris Rock's observation about Shaq: "Shaq is rich, but the white man who signs his check is wealthy." The players, for their part, pointed to the $3 billion a year that the NBA was getting from NBC (a figure that soared to $4.3 billion when the rights were spread among three networks). If owners were losing, it was because they were wedded to the old-fashioned franchise manner of running a sports league.

Their remedy? A hard salary cap and an end to guaranteed contracts to keep the NBA's 29-team model functioning. It was clearly a declaration of war, one that the players could not remedy in the courts. The previous labor disputes had been ended before they could threaten a season. But with the O'Neal deal resonating in their minds, owners imposed a lockout that stretched into the next calendar year, canceling the All-Star Game and threatening to emulate baseball's 1994 example of scrapping the playoffs. They were aided when an arbitrator ruled that teams did not have to pay players with guaranteed contracts during the lockout.

In December 1998, with three months of games canceled, Commissioner Stern said if a deal was not reached by January 7, 1999, the entire year would be canceled. This had the effect of splintering the union's highly paid players (who had most to lose) from the rank and file. At a rancorous meeting on January 6, 1999, O'Neal proposed a secret ballot while others suggested just going back to work while negotiations continued. Others vowed to fight on to the bitter end to resist owner encroachments on their hard-won collectively bargained benefits. Faced with a fractured union, the NBPA went back to bargaining with the NBA.

The talks produced a new six-year CBA. Once more the NBA would be a groundbreaker in the field of salary caps. The league became the first major sports organization to limit the salaries of its players, capping them at between $9 million and $14 million. A rookie pay scale was introduced, pay raises under the Larry Bird exception were restrained and a luxury tax was introduced. It was considered a major win for the NBA, and the gains would embolden owners in other pro sports leagues. They had seen how unions would buckle under enough pressure and, as hockey fans would see in the 2004–05 NHL lockout, collapse completely when stars and journeymen in a union argued about whose benefits were being served.

The NBA was also hoping to get their fans back quickly after denying them their heroes for half a season.

But attendance was down 2 percent across the league once the 1998–99 season resumed. Ticket sales fell nearly 2 percent further in the opening months of 1999–2000 and remained under 17,000 per game for the following three seasons. The league also saw television ratings drop for three consecutive seasons after the lockout. Eventually, however, fans recovered, and O'Neal in Los Angeles was a major factor in the revival.

While the NBPA was dealt a blow by owners and by public opinion, O'Neal thrived in Los Angeles. Teamed with Kobe Bryant, he won three NBA championship rings (a fourth came in Miami in 2006), three playoff MVPs, the 2000 NBA MVP and received annual All-Star berths. His business opportunities expanded along with his on-court accomplishments. By the end of his 19-year-career, O'Neal had earned $292 million in salary and probably more than that from endorsements. Until his final years in Boston and Cleveland, he was the bell cow for NBA salaries, commanding the maximum allowed under the CBAs.

But he'd always be seen as one of the players whom owners used to make their demands for a stringent salary cap. While Shaq's ability to earn was unhurt, the hard caps and salary maximums brought in during his reign as the top player in the league would soon begin eliminating the "middle class" veteran player in the NBA and the other team sports using salary caps in North America.

1.9 ALEX RODRIGUEZ

The post-1990 NBA lockouts — "tall millionaires versus short billionaires," in the words of writer Tony Kornheiser — and the NHL labor stoppages of those same years did little to chasten either players or owners from their destructive labor behaviors. But the sport of baseball was doing all it could to never test the loyalty of its fans again. The 1994–95 strike by players soured a generation of fans for years on the sport. It led, eventually, to the destruction of the Montreal Expos, who were favored to win the canceled World Series of 1994. It also encouraged MLB to look in the other direction when performance-enhancing drugs (PEDs) precipitated a season-long home-run derby later in the decade.

Make no mistake. In 1995, the sides remained as deadlocked as ever over the percentage of revenues that players should take home and how much free agency was too much. Yet both sides recognized that tarnishing the national pastime over salary caps had to end. While the NBA, NHL and NFL would subject their fans to interruptions of play to haggle about billions of dollars, baseball would, to the present day, not resort to strikes or lockouts. Tellingly, in 2016, it reached a new CBA with little public acrimony or threat to lock out or strike. Of all the ownership groups, baseball owners would settle for something less than an absolute salary cap to prevent stoppages and to keep the money coming in.

It's hard to exaggerate the risk baseball had run with its loyal fans. Had Alex Rodriguez and a small number of slugging stars not emerged after the 1994 strike, it would have been a very diminished MLB that entered the 21st century. Fortunately for the owners, A-Rod, Barry Bonds, Mark McGwire, Sammy Sosa and Alex Gonzalez arrived to save the sport by bashing home runs at such a prodigious pace that the stadiums left empty during the strike were filled again, and TV people came forward with blank checks to get a piece of the action.

Yes, the entire home-run race was fueled by PEDs. Yes, the public and press suspected something was funny in this sudden outburst of homers that took the record from Roger Maris's 61 in '61 to Barry Bonds hitting 73 in 2001. Yes, owners were desperate to change the topic. But in the short run, it seemed to matter little in the race between Bonds, McGwire and Sosa to smash records. Fans showed up simply to watch the bulked-up sluggers in batting practice.

The euphoria over the moon-shots was music to the ears of cities being asked to build beautiful new ballparks for their hometown MLB teams. After the success of Baltimore's retro Oriole Park at Camden Yards, built in 1992, MLB teams went on a building spree to create revenue-producing stadiums. By 2010, only a handful of stadiums were older than 20 years, and two (Wrigley Field in Chicago, Fenway Park in Boston) were considered national architectural masterpieces that defied replacement.

MLB also lucked out in that its PED infatuation coincided with a revolution in TV rights for cable sports. Until 1980, TV rights had been sold to over-the-air national networks — free TV, in the old term. Even in local markets, there were limited games available for viewing. A fan might see half of his team's games on his TV during a season; radio made up the difference. Only the NFL had significant revenue from national rights fees, as that league sold its rights collectively. In the other sports, while national rights fees were respectable, local and regional TV was the lifeblood. Multiplying these markets was one of the reasons why leagues had expanded like fast food outlets since the 1960s. But the arrival of ESPN changed the dynamic. No one believed that a 24-hour seven-day-a-week sports channel could work. Until it did. That spawned America-wide imitators like SportsChannel, regional networks and NESN; Canada's TSN and Sportsnet; and the U.K.'s Sky Sports.

With ESPN charging customers up to seven dollars a month for its programming, money began to wash through the pro sports leagues. Then the New York Yankees' renegade owner, George Steinbrenner, bought into the idea of owning a stand-alone network that would have all his team's games and those of the New Jersey Nets of the NBA. While cable operators fought like crazy against carrying these new outlets, customers willingly paid the money to support their sports fixation watching the Yankees dominate baseball with four World Series tiles between 1996 and 2000. Eventually most carriers surrendered and took Steinbrenner's YES network in the tristate region.

It was at this lucrative moment for baseball that Seattle shortstop Alex Rodriguez, perhaps the best player ever to enter MLB, became an unrestricted free agent.

A-Rod, as he's come to be known, was the first pick overall in the 1993 MLB amateur draft. Within three years, he was the starting shortstop for the Mariners and second in balloting for the American League MVP with a rare combination of baseball's "five tools," (hitting for average, hitting for power, base running, throwing and fielding) in 1998, he set the record for homers in a season by a shortstop and also joined the 40 homers / 40 stolen bases club. By 1999, he was the youngest player in MLB history to have hit the 100 homers / 100 stolen bases mark. Still, there was disappointment in Seattle for Rodriguez. Despite the presence of Randy Johnson, Edgar Martinez and Ken Griffey Jr., the Mariners and A-Rod could not get to a World Series. It appeared that if Rodriguez wanted to win a title, it would not be in Seattle.

By the end of the 2000 season, Griffey and Johnson had been traded by the Mariners, leaving A-Rod like Shaquille O'Neal in Orlando — a megastar in a smaller market that was having trouble keeping its stars. Also like O'Neal, Rodriguez was now a free agent, represented by one of the most aggressive agents in the business, Scott Boras — who'd never been crazy about the idea of his star client hidden away in the Pacific Northwest. Boras had urged Rodriguez to go back into the amateur draft in 1993 to avoid going to Seattle, and he didn't want Rodriguez to extend his contract with the Mariners. But A-Rod had still made the commitment to the Mariners, signing a contract extension in 1997 rather than leaving at the first possible opportunity.

Now, with Johnson and Griffey gone, the climate was different. In his contract year of 2000, A-Rod had hit 41 homers with 132 RBIs and a .316 batting average. Many believed he had an excellent chance to own the all-time home-run record if he stayed healthy. He could lead a team to a championship in another market with the sort of financial resources Seattle's absentee Japanese ownership did not provide. As well, statistics seemed to indicate that Safeco Field in Seattle was having a negative effect on his production. In 2000, Alex hit .306/.414/.573 in Safeco and .366/.447/.774 on the road.

The Mariners initially offered him seven years at $63 million, which would have put him in the top 10 MLB salaries. But by the final year of the deal, that annual average salary of $9 million wouldn't even have been in the top 25 MLB salaries. That was hardly where the best player in baseball should be, said Boras. The Mariners sweetened their offer to eight years at $117.5 million. But it was too little, too late. Seattle was eliminated from the bidding.

Everyone assumed George Steinbrenner's New York Yankees would win the bidding war. With his coffers overflowing from the YES money and his position in the number one market in North America, Steinbrenner had the resources and the willpower to bring Rodriguez to the Big Apple. But problems emerged. One issue was that the Yankees already had an iconic shortstop in Derek Jeter. Plus the Yanks had also just won four of the previous five World Series. That necessitated paying the players he already had their high market values. So the wild auction Boras was planning might get too rich even for Steinbrenner.

While Rodriguez considered other factors, Boras convinced A-Rod that he needed to go with the highest bidder — if only to establish a benchmark for the rest of the MLB players to use. That's where Texas owner Tom Hicks came into the scene. A newbie to sports ownership who'd made his fortune as a leveraged buyout specialist, Hicks had purchased the NHL Dallas Stars in 1995. Winning the Stanley Cup in 2000 with the Stars was not enough to satisfy his urge to be a major player in the sports world. So Hicks purchased the Rangers from a group that included future U.S. president George W. Bush. Flush with cable money from his newly formed regional cable TV network, Hicks made it his quest to add the greatest player in MLB to his stable of acquisitions.

Even though the Atlanta Braves, Chicago White Sox, Colorado Rockies, Los Angeles Dodgers and A-Rod's boyhood favorites, the New York Mets, were in the bidding, Hicks would not be dissuaded from creating the largest sports contract in history. Acting as his own GM, Hicks ended up bidding against himself, offering $100 million more than anyone else for A-Rod. The final deal still leaves many staggered: 10 years at $252 million. It was the most an athlete in North America had been paid — a mark that remained unchallenged until Rodriguez himself exceeded it in his 2007 contract extension with the Yankees ($275 million). It took until 2015, when the Florida Marlins gave Giancarlo Stanton 13 years at $325 million, for another athlete to exceed the gross figure of the Texas contract for Rodriguez — and in 2015 dollars.

Rodriguez was good for the money. He delivered for the Rangers in 2001, leading the American League with 52 homers, 133 runs scored and 393 total bases, the first player since 1932 with 50 homers and 200 hits in a season. He was also just the third shortstop to ever lead his league in homers. He followed that with 57 home runs, 142 RBIs and 389 total bases in 2002. He won the American League MVP in 2003 as well as his second Gold Glove in Texas. While the numbers were later tainted by A-Rod's admission that he used PEDs in those years, they are stunning numbers all the same.

Unfortunately for the Rangers, Rodriguez's enormous production did nothing to get Texas to the postseason. And it severely hobbled the Rangers' financial prospects for improving their team. A-Rod had deferred payments stretching to 2025, while Hicks was left scrambling to hang on to the team. In fact, Rodriguez found himself the largest unsecured creditor when Hicks finally took the team into bankruptcy in 2010. That led to a sale to a group that included Rangers legend Nolan Ryan. "I've done some smart things," Hicks told Dallas-CBS affiliate KTVT-TV Channel 11 when asked about Rodriguez. "I've done some dumb things. That was one of the dumb things."

The new ownership group made it crystal clear that no matter how talented Rodriguez was, he was going on the market. Enter Steinbrenner, whose multi-championship squad was now growing old and needed a boost. He had room and — most importantly — the need for a new star. Once he had convinced Rodriguez that his future lay at third base, next to Jeter, the deal went through in 2004, and A-Rod was traded to the Yankees for Alfonso Soriano and Joaquin Arias. Even though Yankee Stadium did little to favor his right-handed hitting, A-Rod won the American League MVP in two of his first four seasons in the Bronx. In a stroke of good timing, A-Rod exercised his right to opt-out of the contract he'd signed in Texas. But nothing with A-Rod is ever so simple. In a stroke of bad timing, Boras announced the opt-out during Game 4 of the World Series between the Boston Red Sox and the Colorado Rockies, earning a rebuke from Major League

Baseball president and CEO Bob DuPuy, "There was no reason to make an announcement last night other than to try to put his selfish interests and that of one individual player above the overall good of the game."

Negotiations grew tense, with the Yankees seemingly walking away from the table. With the public criticizing him for being greedy, Rodriguez was forced to negotiate his new deal without agent Scott Boras. "It seemed like the whole thing was a roller-coaster. It was very emotional," a chastened Rodriguez told reporters on a conference call. "All along, I knew I wanted to be a Yankee." He then admitted that opting out had been "a mistake that was handled extremely poorly . . . It was a huge debacle . . . distasteful and very inappropriate."

However the deal was done, the numbers were no less stunning: 10 years at $275 million for a 32-year-old who was unlikely to ever play out the contract.

While A-Rod and the Yankees won the World Series in 2009, his career in pinstripes was marred by injuries and constant allegations of PED use. Things came to a head when A-Rod was suspended by MLB for the entirety of the 2014 season for the use of PEDs and for engaging in "a course of conduct intended to obstruct and frustrate" the investigation into his PED use and Biogenesis, a lab that supplied PEDs. After he returned from his suspension, A-Rod's role with the Yankees diminished. He moved from being an everyday third baseman to a designated hitter and eventually a pinch hitter.

Things were just as bad off the playing field as on it. A-Rod and the Yankees fought over a $6 million bonus that A-Rod would get for reaching certain milestones in exchange for the Yankees using A-Rod's image rights. When A-Rod got 660 home runs, tying Willie Mays for fourth all-time, one of these bonuses was triggered. The Yankees claimed that A-Rod's image rights did not have any value, based in part on his PED suspension. A-Rod filed a grievance, and the matter was eventually settled, with the Yankees giving $3.5 million to charities.

On August 7, 2016, the Yankees abruptly announced that A-Rod was retiring at the end of the week. In contrast to Derek Jeter's year-long farewell tour, A-Rod was not allowed to even finish out the season, ending his career with 696 home runs. While Rodriguez held out hope that another club, perhaps his hometown Miami Marlins, might give him a last hurrah, the phone never rang again, and he accepted an offer from Fox TV to do analyst work.

When the dust settles on his tumultuous career and personal life, Rodriguez will still be remembered for his prodigious output on the field: a .295 batting average, 3,115 hits, 696 home runs, 2,086 RBIs and 329 stolen bases. His unprecedented contract might have even more resonance across the sports industry. In a business where one contract sets the precedent for the next, A-Rod's contracts were unsurpassed for almost a decade. He showed that great players are worth the money in the proper market.

1.10 DAVID BECKHAM

The business of soccer, at least outside of North America, has a dramatically different structure than the "Big Four" of the NFL, MLB, NBA and NHL. While the North

American leagues largely hitched themselves to a restrictive financial model designed to keep the most teams functioning at the lowest common denominator, soccer in the rest of the world has used a free-market approach in its top leagues, though there have been some restrictions on teams in terms of financial redistribution and more recently in "breaking even" between revenues and spending.

In its purest form, soccer has been about letting the big dogs eat. With few exceptions, the sport has belonged to the markets that could afford the best players in an open market. For many years, this mattered little, as national TV rights and merchandise provided a very small portion of revenues in English, German, Italian or Spanish soccer. The gate was the thing, and so large stadiums in large communities ruled the economic equation.

While North American sports fans believed in the catechism of parity, European fans were content to have great franchises rule. The brutal reality of relegation and promotion allowed the smaller clubs a chance to breathe the rarified air of the top division for a while, but eventually the economic reality took over again, and teams would sink down to their appropriate league. While American leagues were looking to expand a little outside of their northeastern bubble in the 1950s, the Europeans created a series of champions' leagues, the most recent versions being the Union of European Football Associations (UEFA) Champions League and the UEFA Europa League, forming an "elite" level of soccer competition above the regular, domestic leagues.

Perhaps this rampant concentration explains why "the beautiful game" has taken so long to gain a foothold in

North America, where every team believes that, with a little luck, it can grow up to be Super Bowl champ. Perhaps it was the lack of world-class games on TV. Perhaps it was just the kabuki theater of faking injuries that soured North Americans on the world's number one sport. Or perhaps it was the lack of TV time-outs every five minutes, requiring fans to pay attention to the game for 45 minutes just to catch a glimpse of a shot on net, let alone a goal.

But by the 1990s, that was beginning to change. Soccer's notion of stocking the best teams with the best players suddenly appealed to a generation that thought more globally. After several aborted tries at forming a North American league, Major League Soccer seemed to be gaining a toehold not just among immigrant communities but also among longtime North Americans.

Initially, Major League Soccer kept step with the other major leagues, establishing its own salary cap to keep costs down, which it was able to do because all teams were owned by the league itself in what is known as a "single entity" structure that we'll talk about a bit later in the book. However, they also created their own version of the Larry Bird rule in 2007. Called the Designated Player category, it allowed teams to keep a top player or attract a star from Europe, Africa or South America. These Designated Players would count against the cap for only a fraction of what the team was actually paying them. For example, in 2017, a Designated Player would only count for $480,625 against a team's salary cap, regardless of what the actual salary was. MLS made this concession because it understood better than most that star power was the secret to soccer's growing international popularity. In the first decade of the 21st century, there was one player whose star power overcame the North American reluctance to embrace the sport: David Beckham.

Beckham had twice been runner-up for FIFA World Player of the Year. He was inducted into the English Football Hall of Fame in 2008. The 58-time captain of England was named in the FIFA 100 list of the world's greatest living players in 2004.

For most of the fans MLS wanted to capture in the United States, however, he was the eponymous idol of *Bend It Like Beckham*. The film, about a young woman trying to navigate both her culture and soccer, was a surprise hit. The English international star became synonymous with soccer, women's sports and family films. This, in combination with his recent marriage to Victoria, also known as Posh Spice of the Spice Girls, made him a perfect fit for a city like Los Angeles, where the entertainment business is king. Even better, Beckham's agent, Simon Fuller, was, among many other things, the manager of the Spice Girls and the creator of *American Idol*. He was also closely tied to CAA, the dominant L.A. agency in film, music and sport.

It was no accident that destiny chased Beckham. He had always been the golden child of English soccer, signing on at age 14 with the Youth Training Scheme of his boyhood team, the famed Manchester United. He was the under-15 Player of the Year in England and had trained in the school of the famed Man U star Bobby Charlton. In the Reds' system — Sir Alex Ferguson's "school of hard graft" — he developed along with Ryan Giggs, Gary Neville, Phil Neville, Nicky Butt and Paul Scholes. These players would later form the core of Man U's champion clubs of the 1990s, and the 1998–99 United team that would win the "treble" of the Premier League, FA Cup and Champions League.

While playing for United, Beckham won the Premier League title six times, the FA Cup twice and the 1999 UEFA Champions League. Becks came to be known worldwide for his instinctive passing and his ability to make the ball "bend" during his free kicks (hence "bend it like Beckham"). He eventually wore the famed No. 7 jersey worn by Man U legends George Best, Bryan Robson and Eric Cantona, and later by Cristiano Ronaldo. His international career for England was marked by disappointment, however. After debuting with England at the age of 21, he served as captain for six years, never getting England to the final of the World Cup or Euro Championships.

In 2003, he joined Real Madrid as part of the team's "*galácticos*" era, during which similarly major signings occurred every year. In four frustrating years starring at Santiago Bernabéu Stadium, Beckham and his team performed below expectations, winning the La Liga title only after Beckham had agreed to the MLS deal to move to Los Angeles. With age starting to creep up on him, in 2007 Beckham was looking for a soccer challenge and a way to grow the brand he and Victoria were selling around the world.

The Galaxy were owned at that time by Anschutz Entertainment Group, the same company that owned the Kings after Bruce McNall's bankruptcy and imprisonment on fraud charges. Beckham would be more than just another pretty face in a town full of them — MLS hoped that he might be key to luring the growing California Latino community, with its love of soccer, to support the product that they'd so far shunned. Getting Beckham would also fill the luxury boxes with corporate spenders who loved his appeal to the soccer moms. Plus, he already had started a training academy in the city.

Initially, other teams in MLS grumbled about Beckham moving to the Galaxy. As with Bobby Hull's move to the WHA, owners didn't want the charismatic star making their team look weak in front of the home fans. But it didn't take long for them to realize that Beckham could be the gift that kept on giving to all the franchises as they struggled to create a place in their communities. The prospect of a media caravan following the Galaxy around the continent was too good to be true. The international media moved en masse to southern California to cover the English star. Soccer had come of age in the new country.

At a star-studded press conference, it was announced that Beckham's contract was worth $250 million over five years — the largest ever for a team-sport star. In reality, he was only guaranteed $32.5 million in total, or $6.5 million per year. The rest of the money would come by way of marketing and promotional opportunities set up for him. He also received the option of buying an MLS expansion franchise in any market except New York City at the fixed price of $25 million whenever he stopped playing in the league.

Beckham was making more than some entire teams' payrolls in MLS. But MLS had no problem making exceptions to its salary cap for a star like Beckham, creating an entire rule — the Designated Player Rule — just to fit Beckham, and those who would follow him to MLS later on, into the tight salary cap that MLS imposed on the teams.

Getting the Englishman to southern California proved a success for soccer in America, regardless of the price. While he was dogged by injury in his five years in the MLS, Beckham showed the binary value of star power that only soccer could fully exploit at the time. After signing Beckham, the Galaxy inked a new five-year shirt-sponsorship deal with Herbalife worth $20 million. The team gained 11,000 new season-ticket holders and sold out its luxury suites at the Home Depot Center. Media that never touched soccer suddenly produced cover stories on Beckham and his wife. Soccer had begun to go mainstream in North America. After contracting two teams in Florida in 2002, MLS expanded by 10 teams from 2005 to 2012 in response to demand from cities that wanted in.

While his road appearances in the first years were fitful due to injuries and overseas commitments, Beckham became more of a fixture in later seasons, when he returned from training with AC Milan in the MLS off-season. He finished with two strong seasons in L.A., winning the MLS Cup each time, adding his third different league championship to the titles at Man U and Real Madrid. At 36, he decided once more to try European soccer and headed off to finish his career with Paris Saint-Germain.

Beckham made significant contributions on the field, but his lasting legacy was of taking soccer global, breaking free of the traditional club-team bonds. With stars who could be marketed internationally, the regional emphasis of leagues and the relentless expansion model were shown to be a limiting strategy. Soccer was showing that with wireless communications you didn't need a team in every city to be successful. You needed just enough teams to create competition and in which to concentrate the top players. Fans now wanted their entertainers to be cultural figures featured in movies, music and literature as well as being sports stars. Beckham was the first great branded global star.

1.11 LEBRON JAMES

The first indications that North American pro sports might be emulating the global star-driven model pioneered by David Beckham came from the NBA. More specifically, it emerged in the form of LeBron James, the 21st-century incarnation of Michael Jordan as polestar for the league. Even as the NBA continued to expand and promote its traditional salary cap model in CBAs as recently as 2016, James and new superstars such as Steph Curry and Kevin Durant were creating a formula for super-teams that harkened back to the great 1980s Boston Celtics and L.A. Lakers teams that emerged at the beginning of the salary restraints and acrimonious CBA negotiations.

The enormous global popularity of James's Cleveland and Miami teams — as well as Curry's Golden State Warriors — transcended the domestic reach of those famed clubs featuring Bill Russell and Jerry West in the 1960s and '70s. Married to the NBA's participation in the Olympics, James produced a tidal wave of cash for the star players and the league.

Everyone had known that James would be a game

changer if he remained healthy. A man-child at 16, the product of Akron, Ohio, had been a prodigy, with some feeling that he could have played professionally in two, perhaps three sports, like Bo Jackson or Deion Sanders. In his junior year of high school, he made the first of many *Sports Illustrated* cover appearances as the next great superstar prospect. For his senior year, ESPN offered a package to subscribers so they could follow his high-school team, St. Vincent–St. Mary's, as it played around the nation. While every major college basketball program courted James, it was never in doubt that he'd go pro after being drafted number one by the NBA coming out of high school. He even tried, unsuccessfully, to enter the draft coming out of his junior year in high school.

A number of NBA teams did their best to get the top pick in the 2003 draft, but the Cleveland Cavaliers won the right to draft James with a pitiful 17–65 record the season before. While the Denver Nuggets had the same record, the Cavs won the lottery (the Nuggets settled for Carmelo Anthony at the third spot, who would demand a trade to the New York Knicks, which was granted in 2011). A rare combination of power and athleticism at six-foot-eight and 240 pounds, James was also remarkably comfortable with the attention he received when he shook NBA commissioner David Stern's hand as Cleveland's choice in the draft. He instantly became wealthy, not as much from his NBA contract, limited to just over $4 million per year, as from his endorsements. James hit the jackpot in a three-way bidding war among Nike, Reebok and Adidas, signing with Nike for approximately $90 million as he entered the NBA.

While it would be hard to live up to the hype surrounding him, James more than delivered on his promise. He won the NBA Rookie of the Year Award in his first season. By year three, he'd gotten the Cavs back in the postseason for the first time since 1998. In year four, he put on one of the great playoff performances ever, scoring 29 of the final 30 points as Cleveland eliminated the highly favored Detroit Pistons in the Eastern Conference Finals — although the Cavs then lost to San Antonio in the finals.

Then the ascent stalled. While James added personal honors in the form of the NBA MVP in 2009 and multiple All-Star berths, he could not get the Cavs back to the finals, let alone win an NBA title. There was criticism that Cleveland could not or would not add the necessary pieces to make James a champion with the Cavs. Or that LeBron was not a big-game player. While his search for a title was unrewarded in Cleveland, James insisted on signing short-term contracts. In 2006, he negotiated a three-year, $60 million contract extension instead of the four-year maximum, allowing him the option of seeking a new contract worth more money as an unrestricted free agent following the 2010 season (James would not become the highest-paid player in the NBA until 2016).

As he headed to unrestricted free agency in 2010, the pressure began to build. Would James stay in his hometown of Cleveland or succumb to offers from other teams with a better chance to win? Either way, he was about to become fabulously wealthy, with already lucrative advertising and promotional contracts in his pocket. As he walked off the court for the final time in 2010 in

Cleveland, there were boos from fans who felt he'd already decided to leave the franchise and the city, which hadn't seen a major team title since the Browns won the 1964 NFL Championship.

The Chicago Bulls, Los Angeles Clippers, Miami Heat, New York Knicks, New Jersey Nets and Cavaliers were considered the primary teams bidding for James that summer. He told the clubs he'd announce his decision on a nationally telecast special called *The Decision*, on July 8, 2010. But the tip-off came the day before, as both Chris Bosh and Dwyane Wade, who'd played with James on Team USA at the Olympics, said they were going to sign deals in Miami. It became clear that the trio were coordinating a super-team to win the NBA title.

They would coordinate their salaries to remain beneath the salary cap while leaving some money to recruit other talented role players. Another key factor in James moving south was the presence of highly respected Miami president Pat Riley. Sure enough, when *The Decision* was aired, James told host Jim Gray, "I'm taking my talents to South Beach." His six-year, no-trade deal was also under the league's maximum salary, so the Heat could keep Wade, Bosh and a strong enough bench to win.

To say the news that James would be basking by Biscayne Bay the next winter was poorly received back in snowy Cleveland would be an understatement. Cavs owner Dennis Gilbert bitterly responded in a letter to ticket holders (in Comic Sans): "As you now know, our former hero, who grew up in the very region that he deserted this evening, is no longer a Cleveland Cavalier. This was announced with a several day, narcissistic, self-promotional build-up culminating with a national TV special of his 'decision' unlike anything ever 'witnessed' in the history of sports and probably the history of entertainment . . . You simply don't deserve this kind of cowardly betrayal."

But from James's point of view, he was running a race against time, and a Miami team with players he'd helped recruit gave him the best chance to win the NBA title. This flew in the face of the traditional model in pro team sports, where clubs built slowly through the draft for years before contending. Like Beckham at Man U, James in 2010 was impatient with the traditional models. And he embraced his role as the bad boy on his first visit to Cleveland, returning to score 38 points and lead Miami to a win — all the while being booed every time he touched the ball. James later expressed regret, saying before the 2011–12 season: "If the shoe was on the other foot, and I was a fan, and I was very passionate about one player, and he decided to leave, I would be upset too about the way he handled it."

Without LeBron, the Cavaliers disintegrated as a credible basketball team. They finished the next year at the bottom of the Eastern Conference, going 19–63. The next three years were not much better, as the team won 21, 24 and 33 games. The Cavs did have some luck, winning the draft lottery in 2013 and improbably again in 2014, when they had a 1.7 percent chance of doing so. Each time, the Cavs selected a Canadian first overall — Anthony Bennett and Andrew Wiggins. Both players were traded in 2014 as part of a package for Kevin Love in a three-way trade between Cleveland, Minnesota and Philadelphia — and as part of LeBron's homecoming, which we'll get to in a moment.

While Cavs fans lamented LeBron's move to Miami, the media gobbled it up. Even here, the paradigm was unique to LeBron: ESPN assigned one reporter, Brian Windhorst, to cover James exclusively. Let others follow the team; ESPN wanted the sizzle of a superstar. The Heat were also to be featured on national TV broadcasts at every opportunity, becoming a fixture on the NBA's annual high-profile Christmas Day games. Merchandise for the Heat skyrocketed around the globe, with James's no. 6 jersey bringing hundreds of millions of dollars to the NBA. James, too, became a global brand. In 2013, he surpassed Kobe Bryant as the highest-paid basketball player in the world, with earnings of $56.5 million in both salary and endorsements (the $42 million in endorsements making up the lion's share).

In 2015, James was ranked the sixth-highest earning athlete of any kind and third-highest in 2016 (after Cristiano Ronaldo and Lionel Messi). His exclusive deal with Fenway Sports Group gave him a small piece of Liverpool FC in the premiership. And his small investment in Beats headphones brought him $30 million more when the company was sold.

The Heat's star-driven super-team approach almost achieved its goal in year one in Miami. After a shaky start, the Heat found their stride heading into the 2011 playoffs. The dynamic combination of James and Wade — augmented by Bosh — led the Heat to a 2–1 game lead over Dallas in the finals. But then the team came unglued, allowing the Mavericks to win the crown in six games. Many took satisfaction that the preordained championship was denied James after his star-driven defection from Cleveland.

It was only a small setback, however. Powered by James's back-to-back MVP performances, the Heat won two consecutive championships in 2012 and 2013. They'd have made it a three-peat had it not been for the Spurs, who once more tripped up LeBron in six games to win the Larry O'Brien Trophy in 2014.

By this fourth consecutive finals appearance, it was apparent that the Heat's formula for success was coming undone. Wade and Bosh were often injured or ill. Riley was pulling back to let coach Erik Spoelstra handle the team. With this transition from a great team to just a very good one, James craved another epic challenge: finally bringing a title to his hometown of Cleveland. After the acrimony of his departure, this seemed hard to swallow for Cavs fans. But James admitted his regrets over how he'd left (though not the leaving itself), and to the amazement of all made his way back again to northeast Ohio in 2014. As he had done in Miami, James made the acquisition of complementary players a condition of his return. This would be no nostalgia tour but perhaps a final chance to win the NBA championship for Cleveland.

There would be no accusations of the Cavs going cheap this time, as the club, which already had budding superstar point guard Kyrie Irving, added All-Star forward Kevin Love. As in Miami, James was part of a trio of stars sharing the burden of winning. He signed another short deal, a two-year contract worth $42.1 million, with an option to become a free agent again in 2015 — when the

NBA salary cap was expected to rise significantly thanks to the efforts of players like James in making the NBA a huge TV attraction.

As in Miami, the first year fell short of James's expectations. While the remade Cavs made the finals in year one, injuries to Irving and Love left James as the focus of the Cleveland offense. As a result, the hot-shooting Steph Curry and his teammates on the Golden State Warriors took the title in six games over Cleveland. In 2016, however, the Cavs were healthy for the rematch against the Warriors, who'd won a record 73 games in the regular season. James had reportedly engineered the demise of coach David Blatt in midseason, having his friend Tyronn Lue replace him. The move paid dividends. This time it was the Warriors who took a 3–1 series lead in the finals. But James rallied the Cavs to three straight wins, including a triple-double in Game 7. Cleveland had its first major-league championship in 54 years. James was unanimously named the playoff MVP.

The significance of James lies not only in his dominating performances on the court. His trilogy of finals with the Warriors (the Warriors won in 2017), who were building their own super-team with Curry, Klay Thompson, Draymond Green (and, in 2016, Kevin Durant), demonstrated that the NBA doesn't need 30 winning teams to prosper. Network TV contracts, predicated on showcase teams like the Cavs and Warriors, have exploded in value, pushing the NBA salary cap from $63.997 million in 2014–15 to $94.143 million in 2016–17. The networks aren't paying for the Milwaukee Bucks or Utah Jazz. They want the teams that sell beyond the diehard fans in North America. The NBA, like other leagues, needs fewer partners and a smaller upper tier of teams. To do that, it needs to abandon its salary-cap fetish.

PART 2

SPORTS AND THE LAW:
THE FINE PRINT

The first part of this book discussed the business reasons why professional team sports created the salary-cap model that now governs so much of pro sports. To understand why the salary cap is impacting the quality of competition, it's important to understand the structure owners put into place to save themselves from themselves, and how the law prevents them from going further.

Professional sport is a completely different beast than it was during the time of Babe Ruth. On the one hand, players today have rights Ruth could only dream of: guaranteed contracts (except in the NFL), the exercise of free-agency rights and being paid well enough that they don't need off-season jobs to make ends meet — like the one that NHLer Eddie Shack had in the 1960s, selling hats in Manhattan to supplement his $7,500 annual salary. Once their playing careers are over, today's players may even be able to retire without working another day to support themselves.

On the other hand, there are similarities with how sports leagues operated back in the 1920s. Owners still exert near-total control over where players play for the early part of their careers. They can trade players to another city without the players' consent (unless a star negotiates a no-trade or no-movement clause), and they continue to seek ways and means to limit the salaries of players. Often, owners escape media scrutiny for these tactics, as players are still seen in the eyes of the public as getting paid too much to "play a kids' game."

The contracts outlined in the first half of the book demonstrate the erosion of the owners' power and the rearguard actions they employed to deal with the fallout each time the courts forced them to comply with labor law. The owners found out that, while they often had the upper hand, they lacked a completely free hand in implementing new systems to cover up the perceived problems with the player contracts that the owners themselves had drafted.

The actions of team owners were, and remain, ultimately constrained by two legal regimes — antitrust law and labor law (or "competition law" and "labour law" in Canada). To understand how the salary cap and other restrictions, such as the entry draft and limits on free agency, can exist in the first place, it is helpful to have a basic understanding of both of these areas of law. Bear with us here — we'll make it as painless as possible.

2.1 HOW ANTITRUST/COMPETITION LAW WORKS IN SPORTS

Antitrust law is an area that broadly applies to the economy as a whole — and this includes sports leagues, as courts regularly have to remind the leagues. One of the basic ideas in a capitalist economy, like the one we have had in North America for centuries, is competition. Where multiple businesses that sell the same product compete against each other in a marketplace, two beneficial things happen: businesses compete by improving the quality of their goods, spurring innovation; and businesses compete by adjusting the price of their goods, lowering the cost to consumers. Businesses need to offer the highest-quality items at the lowest possible price to attract and retain customers. Businesses that fail to be innovative in the face of challenges will die out, replaced by others that are more competitive.

Antitrust law generally does two things. First, it either prohibits or restricts monopolies. If there is only one business in a particular market, there is a higher chance that anticompetitive practices harmful to consumers will occur. Second, antitrust law prohibits "collusion" by businesses in a particular market. Businesses are not allowed to get together to, say, set prices at a particular level, or promise not to buy from a certain supplier. These anticompetitive agreements harm consumers and other businesses.

Where there is only one, or only a few, major players in a marketplace, businesses do not need to compete as fiercely, since consumers have fewer options. At best, businesses will remain stagnant, not innovating or competing on price. At worst, businesses will take advantage of consumers by raising prices beyond what would otherwise be tolerated by consumers. For instance, imagine that an airline ticket from Los Angeles to New York will cost $500 in a competitive market. Airlines want to attract passengers but need to make some profit, and $500 happens to be the best of both worlds. However, imagine that the airlines got together and agreed that the ticket from Los Angeles to New York would now cost $2,000, for any airline. The airlines make a lot more money; the consumer pays for it. If the consumer doesn't want to pay $2,000, their options are taking a bus or not traveling at all. Antitrust law tries to stop these types of practices.

Monopolies not only may fix prices for consumers but may also reduce wages paid to employees. In a perfect market, businesses compete for the best employees and will pay employees enough to keep them from changing jobs. Returning to the airline example, imagine that airlines agreed that all airline pilots would only get paid minimum wage. So if someone wants to work as an airline pilot, after undergoing thousands of hours of training, their only options will be to work for minimum wage or find a different job.

These antimonopoly arguments are why player unions continued to challenge the leagues in court to get concessions in collective bargaining. Sports leagues are partnerships among the 30 to 32 owners of individual teams.

They organize things like schedules, game rules and who can be in the league. They also set out restrictions like the reserve clause, the draft and the salary cap.

Antitrust law comes into play in sports leagues in two ways. First, these leagues are essentially monopolies. The NHL is the only top-end professional hockey league in the U.S. or Canada. The same goes for the NBA, NFL, MLB and MLS. If you want to be a professional athlete in one of these sports, you only have one option, unless you want to go overseas to Europe, Russia, China, Japan or further afield.

Second, since players sign with teams (except in Major League Soccer, where players sign with the league), the teams should be in competition for the best players. Wouldn't every team like to have a shot at signing Sidney Crosby or Connor McDavid? However, the entry draft, the salary cap and restrictions on free agency are examples of collusion between teams to restrict the competition for Crosby and the best players. Teams organize as a league and create these restrictive rules that limit where players can play upon entering the league (the draft), how players can have teams compete for their services (free agency) and how much players can earn (the salary cap). Doing so effectively reduces the amount teams pay to players than they otherwise would if they competed in the open market. Needless to say, these rules are anticompetitive.

How does that jive with antitrust laws? First, a little background. The first significant consideration of antitrust law's relation to sports was to baseball. The American League and National League are so-called because they used to be separate leagues, often having teams in the same city. The two leagues would poach each other's players — two of whom, Nap Lajoie and Hal Chase, are discussed earlier in this book. The two leagues signed a National Agreement stipulating that each league would honor the other's contracts, putting an end to the poaching. A third league, the Federal League, wanted in on this agreement, but the American and National Leagues denied its wish. The Federal League struck back in court, claiming that the National Agreement was a violation of U.S. antitrust law.

In the Curt Flood story, his case made its way to the Supreme Court to challenge the 1922 decision that baseball was not interstate commerce. The justices in 1922 decided that baseball teams catered to a local market, selling tickets, hot dogs and beer to locals. This finding was vital to the victory of the American and National Leagues, because American antitrust law only applies to interstate commerce, not to local (or intrastate) business. Even though teams had to travel to other cities, this was deemed a "mere incident," and the "exhibition" of baseball "would not be called trade of commerce." The court also found that baseball did not involve the "production" of anything — video highlights and ubiquitous team merchandise being a long way off — and could not be subject to antitrust law. This case created the dreaded "antitrust exemption" for baseball that carries through to this day.

Baseball's antitrust exemption meant that activities that would normally be seen as anticompetitive, such as the reserve clause that troubled Flood so much, could not be challenged under antitrust law. The courts feared that ending the exemption might harm the national pastime, and crucially, the justices wanted Congress to be the ones to risk public wrath by eliminating the exemption.

Other leagues were not as lucky as baseball. In the 1950s and '60s, courts held that other sports leagues were subject to antitrust law. Courts recognized that teams had to travel across state lines, and modern communications had changed the nature of the business. In 1957, the Supreme Court found in *Radovich v. NFL* that "a specific claim is made that radio and television transmission is a significant, integral part of the [NFL's] business, even to the extent of being the difference between a profit and a loss." Because of this, the courts could no longer ignore the business aspect of sport. They held that professional sports had to be regulated in a similar manner to other businesses. As we have already seen, a number of practices carried out by leagues are violations of the competition laws that affect other businesses in both the U.S. and Canada.

The salary cap, in particular, is an example of teams colluding to set a maximum price on players, ensuring that, no matter what a particular player might be worth, they can only earn a certain amount. All of these provisions have been challenged by players in court through the past decades. So the question is, why do these practices remain?

Put simply, the players themselves traded away these rights in exchange for other benefits in collective bargaining. See, that wasn't so bad, was it?

2.2 IF THE SHOE FITS: LABOR LAW APPLIED TO SPORTS

Labor law seems an odd fit with sports, but it is just as important as competition law in understanding how professional sports leagues are shaped today. This is for two reasons. First, it gave the players the power to organize and negotiate with teams. Second, collective bargaining provides an answer to the antitrust problem faced by leagues.

Labor law governs collective bargaining between employees — represented by their union — and employers. The number of employees in private-side unions in both Canada and the United States has been declining over the past decades. In Canada, just over 30 percent of employees belong to a union, while the number hovers around 10 percent in the United States. Most people assume that unionized employees are working-class folks making a modest living, but a large proportion of union members in recent years have been public service employees and teachers — both politically powerful lobbies.

Professional team sports is one of the few industries where unionization remains the norm. This is counterintuitive, seeing as how these union workers make millions of dollars. But as we saw in part 1 of this book, it wasn't always that way.

Players in a number of sports had attempted to organize for decades before successfully doing so in the 1950s and '60s. In 1885, baseball players formed the Brotherhood of Professional Baseball Players, aiming to combat the reserve clause and to fight for an increase in player salaries. John Montgomery Ward, a player who also happened to be a lawyer, led the organization of the union. While the National League owners recognized the Brotherhood in 1887, negotiations were fraught with difficulty — as they often have between employers and sports unions. The impasse in negotiations led to the creation of the Players' League in 1890. The teams in the Players' League were owned and operated by the players themselves. However, the league was short-lived, folding the next year, and the Brotherhood faded away not long after.

While the Brotherhood was unsuccessful as a result of owner intransigence, other attempts at unionization were met with much more open hostility by the owners. In the NHL of 1956, "Terrible" Ted Lindsay was a member of Detroit's famed "Production Line" with Gordie Howe and Sid Abel, scoring 30 goals and 75 points in 70 games. That year, Lindsay was stripped of his captaincy on the team. In the summer of 1957, he was suddenly traded to the struggling Chicago Black Hawks, along with Glenn Hall, for Hank Bassen, Forbes Kennedy, Bill Preston and Johnny Wilson. What caused Lindsay's value to the team to drop off so much that the Red Wings had to get rid of him?

He attempted to form a players' association — a union.

Feeling he was near the end of his career, Lindsay had become curious about the NHL players' pension plan. The NHL refused to give Lindsay any information, and so Lindsay sought to form a players' association to better organize to obtain information. By trading Lindsay, the Red Wings — and the NHL — had hoped to discredit the union drive. While the NHL's plan to suppress union activity in its sport succeeded in the short term, the players were eventually able to form the NHL Players' Association in 1967. Unfortunately for the players, the NHLPA turned out to be a house union with a leader sympathetic to the owners until almost 1990. When the NHLPA was founded, it became the last of the recognized team sports unions (the NBPA had started operations in 1954, the NFLPA in 1956 and the MLBPA became a recognized union in 1966).

The first thing that unions did was provide players with negotiating power. As we saw with Babe Ruth, individual players had traditionally negotiated their salaries with their teams on their own. While Babe made out just fine, the rest of his colleagues were crushed underfoot. During the pre-union period, when the teams were able to enforce the reserve clause, contract negotiations were a sham. Players faced the choice of accepting the wage offered by the team or not playing at all (and hoping that the team wouldn't call their bluff). The evolution described in part 1 shows the extraordinary lengths players went to before they finally got a fair shake in negotiations.

Even as the reserve clauses were slowly dismantled and the unions flourished, players were still at a disadvantage. This disadvantage was a lack of information among the players. How much money did the teams make? How much were the players really being paid? No one knew, and no single player could overcome this lack of information. It's like buying a car if the dealer knows the value of all of the possible cars, and you have no idea how much a car is worth and can't compare to other cars.

This lack of information affected players such as

Red Wings legend Gordie Howe. Howe was one of the best players of his era, if not the best, and was frequently assured by Detroit Red Wings owner Bruce Norris and general manager Jack Adams that he was being paid like it. During the 1968–69 NHL season, Howe scored 44 goals and 103 points at the age of 40. And he probably felt he had earned every penny of his $45,000 annual salary.

That summer, the Red Wings brought in defenseman Carl Brewer. Shortly afterwards, Howe found out that not only was he not the highest-paid player in the game, he was only the third-highest-paid player on the team, behind Brewer and Bobby Baun — who were both being paid much more than Mr. Hockey. Howe turned his business affairs over to his wife, Colleen, and confronted Norris. Norris eventually increased Howe's salary to $100,000 per year. The story goes that Howe accosted Norris: "Here I've been playing all these years for you, and you just give me that now?" with Norris replying, "Gordie, you never asked for anything more. I'm a businessman."

Howe would later experience the same stalemate when he discovered that his pension after 25 NHL seasons was a meager $13,000 a year.

Why couldn't the best player in the game become the highest-paid player on his team? Moreover, how could he not have known? Part of the explanation comes from the power disparity between the team and the player. But just as much can be explained by Howe's lack of information. For years, he was told by corrupt NHLPA director Alan Eagleson that salary disclosure among players was harmful. Eagleson said jealousies would emerge when players knew how much their teammates made. Better to keep quiet and maintain harmony in the dressing room. It was not until the early 1990s that NHL players and their agents got the right to hear what others made. Armed with comparable salaries, they quickly made huge gains in their compensation.

Today, thanks to the efforts of their unions, all players — and all fans — know how much other players make. Players can compare themselves to other players, and to their salaries, as they negotiate — and can more effectively make their case. Fans can also see what the management of their team spends and whether or not they are managing the cap wisely — meaning that fans can better hold management accountable for a team's performance.

However, even 50 years after Howe's shocking discovery, owners are still reluctant to let information like player salaries be made public. From 2009 to 2015, the website CapGeek kept track of NHL player salaries and their effects on the salary cap. The website was valuable not only for fans to keep tabs on their teams but was also used by several teams for their own calculations. In early 2015, founder Matthew Wuest closed the site as he fought what was eventually a losing battle with cancer. Shortly after the closing of CapGeek, in February 2015, NHL commissioner Gary Bettman was questioned about whether, as part of the NHL's new "advanced stats" package created in partnership with technology firm SAP, they would provide the type of salary-cap information provided by Wuest's CapGeek. Bettman's evasive response was telling: "I don't think it's a resource we need to provide, because I'm not sure fans are as focused on what players make as they are about their performance on the ice." Bettman's attempts to put the genie back in the bottle have failed so far, as other websites have sprung up to carry on Wuest's work.

Unionization also gave players the power to strike. Considering what using the threat of labor stoppage has done for players, it's hard to imagine the resistance players had to using the weapon. Baseball players in the 1960s worried about being branded as communists when union leader Marvin Miller broached the topic. Many were concerned (rightly, it turned out) that they'd be shunned in their hometowns by fans deprived of their favorite sport. Some experienced their worst abuse from family members who thought they were throwing away their careers. This is to say nothing of the criticism they received from traditional sports reporters in the pocket of owners.

The advent of the player agent also had a huge impact on players getting fair compensation and understanding their collective power via the union — which is probably why the leagues and owners fought so hard to keep agents away from the athletes. While agents fought viciously among themselves for clients, they were able to unite to take advantage of salary disclosure and labor law to help their players. As a general manager will explain, the agent has just one file to master in any negotiation; the GM has anywhere from 25 to 55 contracts to juggle. The agent can concentrate in greater detail to get what he wants from the single negotiation. In addition, the agent has a direct incentive to obtain the best deal for his client. An agent takes a percentage of the salary he negotiates — although it is often limited by the relevant players' association. For instance, agents who represent NFL players cannot receive more than 3 percent of a player's salary. This means that the agent has an incentive to negotiate a larger payday for his client if he wants to make more money for himself.

Agents can also undermine the union, if they are strong enough. As described in the Shaquille O'Neal chapter, a few powerful agents such as David Falk effectively crippled the NBPA during the lockout of 1995 and were influential during the 1998–99 lockout. In the NFL, agents such as Lee Steinberg guided their star quarterbacks into exclusive marketing deals with the league, taking a significant revenue source from the NFLPA. And Alan Eagleson began his rise to the head of the NHLPA by negotiating Bobby Orr's first contract with the Boston Bruins.

You might be thinking: aren't CBAs between employees and an employer are a form of collusion? Yes, they are. The collusion occurs as employers and employees create restrictions on competition — most commonly in wages, as employees are slotted into a "lock-step" system where employees make a certain amount of money and move up the salary scale every year. In this system, individual negotiation for wages is often impossible (sports being the one exception). But there may also be restrictions on who can enter the workforce — for example, requiring certain qualifications for a job.

Legislators and courts realized that the entire bargaining system would fall apart if collective agreements were considered to be collusive activities that violated competition law. Without going into too much detail, most items agreed to in a collective bargaining agreement cannot be subjected to competition-law scrutiny. If the parties agreed to the restriction, it would be counterproductive for a court to allow one party to then claim that the agreed provision violated competition law. This is why, in nasty negotiations, sports-labor unions such as the NFLPA and NBPA decertified. Saying that a union no longer existed removed the protections of labor law from the leagues, leaving them vulnerable to antitrust claims and the potential of crippling "treble damages." Oddly enough, sports is perhaps the only industry where owners *benefit* from employees' being in a union, as much as they dislike the strength of organized players.

2.3 THE ENTRY DRAFT

Other collusive activities are allowed in professional team sport. Take the amateur drafts that leagues have used to distribute incoming talent since the 1930s. The entire concept of the draft is anticompetitive, because it prevents players from negotiating with whatever team will take them. Instead, players can only negotiate their contracts with the team that drafted them, and they are often limited to "rookie wage scales," limiting what they can actually bargain for. As we'll see, this exclusivity has led to teams "tanking" to get access to a generational player such as Connor McDavid or Auston Matthews making things not only legally anticompetitive, but also anticompetitive in a sporting sense.

Rules around draft eligibility are clearly anticompetitive, too. For instance, the NBA today requires that players be out of high school for at least one year, while the NFL mandates prospective players finish three years of college football. Why? The system forces basketball players to play for at least one year in the college system, where they will not get paid and will not finish their education. The league argues that players need time to mature physically and psychologically. However, Moses Malone, Kobe Bryant and LeBron James were all drafted out of high school and were immensely successful.

The contradictions within the draft system were first challenged in the U.S. courts in 1970. Oregon defensive back Yazoo Smith was a 1968 first-round pick of the Washington Redskins. After his career was cut short by a neck injury, he challenged the NFL draft as an anti-competitive act and a violation of U.S. antitrust law. An appeals court agreed with Smith (he was awarded treble damages in the amount of $276,600) and found that the draft could not be justified. The NFL quickly reached an agreement with the NFLPA to protect the draft under a collective bargaining agreement.

In 1987, Leon Wood challenged the NBA Draft in the courts. Wood was drafted by the Philadelphia 76ers in the first round of the 1984 draft. Unlike the recent sad-sack Sixers, the 76ers of the 1980s were spending up to the salary cap. In fact, they were spending so much that their payroll exceeded the salary cap. To keep Wood's rights, the 76ers offered him a one-year, $75,000 contract. Wood took his case to the courts, claiming that the college draft, the salary cap and other restrictions were a violation of antitrust law. An appellate court dismissed Wood's claims because the draft and salary cap were collectively bargained and therefore covered by the exemption to antitrust law provided by labor law.

The draft's age restrictions have also been challenged. In 1976, Ken Linseman, later known as "the Rat," challenged the World Hockey Association's draft rules that required players to be 20 years old. A court found that these restrictions, which were not collectively bargained, were violations of antitrust law.

Almost two decades later, NFL age restrictions were challenged, but with less success. Maurice Clarett had a breakout season for the Ohio State Buckeyes in 2002, becoming the first freshman to start at running back for Ohio State since 1943 and helping the Buckeyes to an undefeated season and the national championship. Clarett was soon embroiled in scandal, fighting with coaches, under investigation for academic misconduct, and was suspended for the 2003 season after being charged with filing a false police report. Clarett wanted to enter the NFL but was blocked by the rule that players must be three years out of high school to be eligible for the draft.

Clarett sued the NFL, claiming that the three-year restriction was an "unreasonable restraint upon the market for players' services." He argued that he was qualified to play pro football and that the age restriction was an arbitrary restriction on his ability to sell his services to NFL teams. Although a federal judge initially agreed with Clarett, the Second Circuit Court of Appeals did not. The appeal court ruled that, since the restriction was part of the collective bargaining agreement between the players' union and the NFL, it was not subject to antitrust law and was therefore legal. This is even though Clarett had no role or representation in the union, as the union was made up of current players who sought to protect their own jobs.

After the decision by the Court of Appeals, Clarett did enter the NFL draft in 2005. Surprisingly, he was drafted in the third round by the Denver Broncos. Following his showing up to training camp overweight, and fights with coaches, Clarett was released before playing a single down in the NFL.

Some challenges to the structure of the draft did not involve the courts. In 1987, Eric Lindros was a heralded player coming out of junior hockey in Oshawa. But he balked at the idea of going to the sad-sack Quebec Nordiques. The small French-language market would restrict his marketing opportunities. But Lindros received no sympathy from either the NHL or the NHLPA, which had negotiated away his rights to a free market coming into the NHL.

With no legal options, Lindros used his only alternative — he refused to report to Quebec, spending the year in junior hockey and with the 1988 Canadian Olympic hockey team. Despite the pressure on him to accept the established system, Lindros held out for almost a year. Just before the 1988 NHL draft, Lindros got his way. Quebec traded him to Philadelphia, where he became a Hall of Famer. But the NHL's system was still intact, and no player has tried to emulate Lindros since then.

Other players have also forced trades following the draft. In the NFL, John Elway used the same holdout threat to force a trade away from the Baltimore Colts, who'd picked the Stanford star QB first in the 1984 draft. Elway went so far as to play pro baseball in the New York Yankees system before the Colts relented, sending him to Denver, where he had a Hall of Fame career. In the NBA, hotshot Steve Francis balked at going to the Vancouver Grizzlies after they selected him in the draft. Francis reluctantly reported to the Grizzlies, but after an incident at the Vancouver airport where he was asked if he and his entourage were a rap group, he soon got his wish, being sent to Houston Rockets in a three-team, 11-player deal.

So how can these restrictions on drafted players be justified by a union? Because undrafted players are not members of the unions yet, the rights of prospects and draftees are often the ones sacrificed in collective bargaining. To get a deal done and not upset veterans, it's easier to put restrictions on the bargaining power of the newcomers who aren't yet union members.

But rookies are generally cheap, since they're young and untested. And the draft robs them of bargaining power. Rookies in the NFL had some leverage, able to negotiate contracts for tens of millions of dollars — the last mega-deal being Sam Bradford's $76 million contract for six years. The NFL moved to limit rookie salaries, assigning the contract value to the draft pick in a lock-step format. No negotiations would be involved, no way for an owner to overpay the next JaMarcus Russell.

But it's a bit different with veteran players. Veterans have free agency, some bargaining power and a track record. But as with rookies, owners couldn't stop themselves from breaking the bank, as we've seen in part 1. So to impose upon themselves some semblance of self-control, owners pushed for a salary cap.

2.4 FREE AGENCY AIN'T FREE

Players can move from one team to another in a few ways, most of which are in the control of the owners. First, players can be traded from one team to another. Players generally have no say over what team they are traded to. Second, players can be "waived." Teams can say, "We don't want this player on our team right now, and whoever wants to pick them up can take them." Third, players can exercise "free agency." In free agency, players can finally compete in a free market for their services once their contract has ended. After several years of playing in a professional league and progressing through various stages of "restricted free agency" (which is often not really free agency at all), players can become "unrestricted free agents."

Players are expected to honor the contracts that they have signed. While under contract to a team, they cannot simply leave that team for another one. However, the same restrictions on movement do not apply to teams — unless a player can negotiate movement protection. A team can trade a player to another team for whatever reason and at whatever value it deems proper. Take Jeff Carter. Carter had just signed an 11-year deal with the Philadelphia Flyers in November 2010. He hoped to remain a Flyer for the rest of his career with this deal, and he was able to negotiate a no-trade clause from 2012 to 2015 and a limited no-trade clause (stipulating that he could only be traded to particular teams) afterwards. The ink was barely dry on the paper when Carter was traded to the Columbus Blue Jackets in the summer of 2011 — before the no-trade clause kicked in. So while the Flyers complied with the letter of the no-trade clause, you could ask if they complied with the spirit. Carter had likely given up salary to get the no-trade clause, and the Flyers shipped him out anyway.

The Flyers gave a number of reasons for the trade, including rebuilding the team, but speculation was rampant that the Flyers were trying to dismantle the party culture of the team by trading away Carter and by sending Mike Richards to the Los Angeles Kings. Carter, disappointed at being traded from a team that had made the Stanley Cup Finals in 2010 to a perennial basement-dweller in Columbus, made his displeasure widely known. After only half a season, the Blue Jackets traded Carter to the L.A. Kings, where Carter became an integral part of the Stanley Cup teams of 2012 and 2014. So while things turned out well for Carter in the end, his story is an example of how loyalty to a team can sometimes be a one-way street.

Before a player becomes a true free agent, they can become a "restricted free agent." If the term "restricted free agent" sounds like an oxymoron, it is. Here is how a restricted free agent can move to another team. First, the team that wants to sign the restricted free agent is required to make an offer. Right out the gate, it is not the player who gets to choose the team but the team that gets to choose the player. If no teams make an offer, then the player will re-sign with their old team. If a team makes an offer, it is up to the player to decide whether to sign the offer. This is where things get interesting. If the player signs the offer, their original team has the right to match the offer. If the team does not match the offer, then the player goes to the new team, and the old team gets compensated — usually in the form of draft picks.

In 2007, one year removed from a Stanley Cup Finals appearance, the Edmonton Oilers were attempting to climb out of the basement of the NHL — an experience that would last for a full decade. The Oilers attempted to sign unrestricted free agents to bolster their team, failing to land forward Michael Nylander, but successfully landing defenseman Sheldon Souray. However, the most controversial move, at least at the time, was to make an "offer sheet" to two restricted free agents — left-winger Thomas Vanek of the Buffalo Sabres and left-winger Dustin Penner of the Anaheim Ducks. Vanek had come off his second NHL season, in which he scored 84 points in 82 games, including 43 goals. He signed the seven-year, $50 million offer sheet from the Oilers, but the Sabres matched, keeping the rights to him. Having lost Daniel Briere and Chris Drury to free agency, the Sabres deemed Vanek too valuable to let go.

Things played out differently with Penner. Penner had just come off his second season in the NHL, scoring 29 goals. The Oilers offered Penner $21.25 million over five years. Penner signed, and the Ducks refused to match. In return for signing Penner, the Oilers had to send three of their draft picks — a first-rounder, a second-rounder and a third-rounder — to the Ducks as compensation.

The signing was controversial in the NHL at the time. It was not controversial for the fact that the Oilers offered $4.25 million per year to a player who had scored almost 30 goals. The simple act of offering a restricted free agent an offer sheet in the first place, let alone two in one summer, was seen as blasphemous by the other general managers. Ducks general manager Brian Burke called the signing "an act of desperation" by Oilers GM Kevin Lowe and said that it was simply Lowe "fighting to keep his job." In response to the draft picks that the Oilers had to surrender, Burke commented: "We're going to take three draft picks back and given Kevin's recent performance, I expect them to be excellent picks." The war of words escalated, with Lowe and Burke threatening to fight each other — in a barn, no less — until NHL commissioner Gary Bettman stepped in to calm tempers.

How did the signing work out for the teams? Penner played almost four full seasons in Edmonton before being traded to the L.A. Kings in 2011. While he was maligned by Oilers fans for looking out of shape and lazy on the ice, he scored 23, 17, 32 and 21 goals for the Oilers in those four seasons — a bright spot on some truly bad teams. As for the draft picks the Ducks got in return for Penner, Burke proved to be wrong. Perhaps the most interesting thing that can be said about them is that with the second-round pick from the Oilers, the Ducks drafted Justin Schultz — a player who was later signed by the Oilers as a free agent before he even played a game for the Ducks.

One year after the Penner offer-sheet signing, two NHL teams made dueling offer sheets. On July 1, 2008, the Canucks offered St. Louis Blues forward and restricted free agent David Backes a three-year, $7.5 million offer sheet, which would have netted the Blues a second-round draft pick as compensation. Only a few hours later, the Blues matched the offer to retain their young forward, who had just come off a 13-goal, 31-point season. Instead of attacking the Canucks in the media, the Blues made their own offer sheet. They made a one-year, $2.5 million offer sheet for Canuck forward Steve Bernier on July 8. Bernier had not even played one single game for the Canucks, who had acquired him from the Buffalo Sabres on July 4. The Canucks quickly matched the offer sheet. Unlike Brian Burke, Mike Gillis, GM of the Canucks, was more sanguine, stating: "I guess quid pro quo is what it is. We were aggressive, and they've been aggressive."

What these stories tell us is that even though there are "restricted free agents" in the NHL, they are rarely actually free agents. Teams seem to expect that restricted free agents will remain with their team — and importantly, that other teams will not exercise their right to try and sign them. Doing so has been controversial among general managers and, as a result, rare. So it seems that restricted free agency is not very valuable to the players.

One thing restricted free agents might get is arbitration rights in some leagues. If a team and a player eligible for arbitration cannot come to an agreement, either party may request that an arbitrator make a decision on what the player should be paid for the next season or two. The team and the player present their cases, with the player trying to pump up his value and the team telling the arbitrator why the player isn't worth what he says he is. The parties will argue over things like statistics, injuries, contribution to the team and leadership, while comparing the player to other players. Naturally, things can get nasty.

One story from 1997 involves New York Islanders GM Mike Milbury — who as a player once hit a fan with their own shoe — and Tommy Salo, the Islanders goaltender (Salo is also remembered for letting in a game-winning goal by Belarus from center ice in the 2002 Olympics). The arbitration went about as well as one could expect, with Milbury ranting to Salo's agent that Salo had poor conditioning and wasn't an NHL-quality goaltender. Salo reportedly left the room, and when he came back, he was in tears. While that relationship was irreparably damaged, Milbury had just drafted goaltender Roberto Luongo (who we'll talk about later) — and traded Luongo away after just one season in an Islanders' uniform.

Mike Johnson was once called "the worst forward in the NHL" by the Phoenix Coyotes in their arbitration brief. To avoid this circus, teams and players often settle the night before or the day of an arbitration hearing. So, needless to say, while arbitration is open to players and teams, they prefer to avoid it if at all possible.

When a player is eligible for unrestricted free agency, once his contract ends, he is not bound to any team. As a result, he can sell his services to the highest, or otherwise most attractive, bidder. Very few players actually become free agents. For instance, NFL players are eligible to become free agents after four years of playing. But, according to the NFLPA, the average NFL career is only 3.3 years. In the NHL, players may become free agents when they turn 27 or have played seven seasons in the league. However, the average NHL career is about five or six seasons, with over half of NHL players tallying less than 100 total games in the league.

But the rarity of true free agents makes them attractive to teams, and they command a premium. For those players who become free agents, selling their talents in an open market to the highest bidder can net millions of dollars — even for mediocre players. So what the system is left with is players who are underpaid when they are young and producing because of a lack of bargaining power, but when players become free agents, teams trip over each other trying to sign them, greatly inflating the players' value and often leading to deals that the team will regret — especially in a salary-capped league. And given that free agents are often signed just as, or just after, they reach their athletic prime, teams are paying for declining productivity.

Albert Pujols should be a warning to any team. In 2011, Pujols was signed for 10 years and $240 million by the Anaheim Angels. Pujols was just about to turn 32, meaning the Angels would be stuck with Pujols until he was 42 (he also had a no-trade clause). The first year in Anaheim, Pujols's game began to decline — and has continued to do so since. His career-low batting average before the free-agent deal was .299 in 2011. Every other year before that, he had been above .310. Since the deal, the best Pujols could manage was .285 in 2012, with the other years between .241 (2017) and .272 (2014). Pujols has been paid an All-Star wage to essentially be just a little bit better than a replacement-level player.

So what happens when a team signs a bad contract like the one given Pujols? Normally, the team would be stuck with the contract. But teams are attempting to do something about that. In this regard, the NFL is seen by other leagues as the gold standard. The NFL is infamous for having "non-guaranteed" contracts. As we saw in part 1, the NFL player contract states that a team can cut a player for a number of reasons, including failure "to establish or maintain his excellent physical condition," deficient "skill or performance . . . compared with that of other players" and "personal conduct reasonably judged by a Club to adversely affect or reflect on Club." In other words, NFL players can be cut free of their contracts for almost any conceivable reason. That is why the "guaranteed" part of player contracts are so important to NFL players.

Other leagues have taken notice and are attempting to eliminate guaranteed contracts in collective bargaining. Teams can now "buy out" contracts. If a team makes a bad signing, it can choose to buy out the player's contract by giving him a portion of his salary to make him go away. Buyouts can help both teams and players. Teams often get some sort of salary-cap relief, while the players get a portion of their contract and can then go play for another team. Remember Thomas Vanek, who the Oilers tried to sign? After six and a half more seasons in Buffalo, he became a bit of a journeyman, going to the New York Islanders and Montreal Canadiens in the 2013–14 season. In the summer of 2014, he signed a three-year, $19.5 million contract. Two years into the deal, the Wild simply bought out Vanek's contract to make room for other free-agent signings.

While free agency is a way for players to get paid what the market will bear, most players never get that chance. Owners often sign free agents to overpriced deals that they learn to regret sooner than later. So they continue to try and come up with more ways either to restrict free agency or to allow them to undo their mistakes — whether through buyouts or non-guaranteed contracts. But since players are unlikely to give up free agency or guaranteed contracts anytime soon, the owners have had to do something else to keep free-agent salaries down. Enter the salary cap.

2.5 SO WHAT THE HECK IS A SALARY CAP, THEN?

As we've seen with the remarkable contracts of the past, the salary cap has adopted different wrinkles in each league. But each cap shares fundamental principles. Put simply, the salary cap is a system that limits the amount that a team can spend on players' salaries in any given year. Salary caps restrict spending in two ways: by limiting the amount that a team can spend on total player salaries, and by limiting the amount that teams can spend on any one player.

The NHL is one such salary-cap league. It took three major labor stoppages for the league to get its cap from the NHLPA in negotiations, with the 2004–05 lockout costing the NHL the entire season. The NHL won its salary cap in 2005 but pushed for another lockout in 2012 to get changes to the cap. So what does it look like? For the 2016–17 season, the NHL had a salary cap of $73 million — which is just a little less than the highest team salary in the pre-salary-cap era, the Detroit Red Wings' $77.8 million in 2003–04. Due to this cap, no team can spend more than $73 million on its entire NHL roster.

In addition to the team cap, individual NHL players

have their own cap. For the 2016–17 season, an NHL player could earn a maximum of $14.6 million per season. No player made that maximum, with the closest being Anze Kopitar of the L.A. Kings, at $14 million per season; Patrick Kane and Jonathan Toews of the Chicago Blackhawks, making $13.8 million per season each; and Montreal Canadien Shea Weber, earning $12 million per season to patrol the Habs blue line. However, these salaries do not necessarily equal the "cap hit." The salary cap hit is calculated by averaging the value of the contract over the course of its lifespan. So while Kopitar made the most money in 2016–17, his cap hit was $10 million, less than the $10.5 million cap hit of Kane and Toews and far more than the $8 million cap hit of Weber. We'll talk more about the distinction between contract value and cap hit a bit later.

In addition to limiting spending, the NHL salary cap mandates that teams spend a minimum amount of money. This is known as the "salary floor." In 2016–17, teams had to spend a minimum of $54 million on player salaries. The small-market Carolina Hurricanes were the closest to the floor, at about $59.5 million.

How do we get these numbers? Salary caps are calculated based on the revenue earned by teams and leagues. For the NHL, the salary cap is at 50 percent of "Hockey Related Revenue," the NFL's salary cap is at about 47 to 48 percent of the NFL's revenue, while the NBA's salary cap is just under 45 percent of "Basketball Related Income." What is included in the "revenue" or "income" of teams is contentiously negotiated by the players' associations and the owners. For instance, the question of what is and is not "Hockey Related Revenue" takes up 20 pages of the NHL's latest collective bargaining agreement. Why is it so contentious?

Once upon a time, operating a sports team was easy. Think of the Charlestown Chiefs in the iconic 1977 movie *Slap Shot*. The Chiefs are a losing team. To keep the fans buying tickets to the games, thereby keeping the team solvent, the Chiefs have to cut all sorts of costs, such as using a cheap bus, and resort to bizarre promotions, such as bringing in the notorious Hanson brothers. The fans only really start coming when the Chiefs begin to play a crazy, violent style of hockey, led by the Hansons. Although it looks like the team will stay afloat, the closure of the nearby mill and the team owner's indifference (she just wants to sell the team as a tax write-off) mean that there is no happy ending.

But making money with a modern sports team is not as simple as putting on a good show at the rink and selling tickets to fans. In addition to tickets, fans buy things like food and drinks, luxury seats, personal seat licenses and merchandise. There are also the things that teams sell to companies, like signage and sponsorships. And that's just inside the arena. Outside of the arena, there's television rights, internet streaming rights and foreign broadcasting rights, among other things. Some of these are easy to categorize as "Hockey Related Revenue," but some are more complicated.

So, what do these revenues consist of at the end of the day? It depends on how they are negotiated. In the NHL, Hockey Related Revenue includes tickets, television and radio broadcasting rights, advertising from team internet sites, a portion of merchandise and concessions, a portion of signage and some parking. Hockey Related Revenue does not include, for instance, fines collected by the league from players for disciplinary reasons. That seems pretty logical. However, it also does not include "Revenues from . . . the grant of any new franchise." Meaning that the $500 million the NHL owners made from awarding the Las Vegas Knights their expansion franchise does not go to the players at all.

One of the most spectacular revenue growth areas is digital rights. When MLB sold BAMTech — a spinoff of MLB Advanced Media — to Disney for $3.75 billion, it meant each team would receive over $50 million in early 2018. None of these revenues are calculated into MLB's revenue sharing agreement with players.

Or, take signage at the home of the Toronto Maple Leafs, Toronto Raptors and countless concerts. Scotiabank took over naming rights in 2018 for $800 million over 20 years — ten times as much as Air Canada paid previously. So how much of the revenue that Scotiabank pays for the naming rights goes into Hockey Related Revenue? It surely cannot be 100 percent to NHL's Hockey Related Revenue and 0 percent to the NBA's Basketball Related Income. How is that naming revenue divided when it comes to calculating salary-cap revenues? It's often a closely guarded secret.

Team owners also have deals that might be related to their ownership of an arena but are not directly related to the team itself. What if a team owner has a restaurant near the arena? Or what if they have a condo develop-ment like the ones surrounding the Scotiabank Centre?

These ventures look less like Basketball or Hockey Related Revenue. Fighting over and figuring out these issues is part of the reason why the collective bargaining agreements are so important and cumbersome.

2.6 EXCEPTIONS TO THE CAP

As with every rule in life, there are people who will comply with the letter and the spirit, and there are those who will test the edges of both. The salary cap has certainly been no different. Touted as a mechanism to put teams on an equal playing field by preventing them from holding on to all of their high-end and high-priced talent, salary caps were imperfectly constructed. No sooner had the salary cap been implemented than the teams sought exceptions or loopholes to exploit.

The most famous exception among fans is the NBA's Larry Bird rule, discussed earlier. This exception to the NBA's salary cap allows a team to re-sign its own player, even if the contract ends up pushing the team over the salary cap, giving teams a better chance to keep their stars. Today, the Larry Bird rule also allows players re-signing with their team to sign a six-year contract, as opposed to the five-year contract that is otherwise the maximum.

The NBA's Bird exception opened the floodgates to a number of other exceptions. The mid-level exception, the bi-annual exception, the rookie exception, the early bird exception, the non-bird exception, the minimum salary exception, the traded player exception, the disabled player exception, and the reinstatement exception

— with all of these exceptions, it's a wonder that the league bothers with a salary cap in the first place.

Major League Soccer has its own formula to, in theory, prevent its owners from blowing the budget for themselves and the competition. The MLS started under the inauspicious shadow of the North American Soccer League (NASL), which was as known for its lavish spending as it was for its disregard of soccer's traditional rules. Spending millions of dollars on aging stars such as Pelé and Johan Cruyff prompted a short-term boost of interest in the league, but it never could recoup the spending, and it shut down in 1984.

MLS began life with a strict cap on player spending, to control costs and to avoid becoming another NASL. MLS was able to enforce such a strict cap out the gate because the league head office, not the teams, negotiates the individual player contracts on behalf of the league's owner and investors. This setup, known as "single entity," rendered MLS immune from antitrust. In other leagues, teams compete to sign players, and a restriction such as a salary cap is collusion among the teams. However, as MLS is the only entity signing the players, it cannot collude with itself. In 2002, a court agreed and found in *Fraser v. Major League Soccer* that MLS is a single entity that can lawfully centrally contract for player services.

Within that salary cap, however, there is a significant exception: the Designated Player Rule, or the "David Beckham rule," as some call it since it was created to get Beckham to MLS. The Designated Player Rule allows a team to sign a player for any value, with only a limited amount charged as the cap hit. The rule has been so popular that teams can now have up to three Designated Player spots. Teams get allocated two spots and can pay a $250,000 fee to MLS (which then gets redistributed among the other teams) for a third.

The Designated Player Rule has allowed teams to sign players for amounts that dwarf the entire salary cap. In 2016, the cap was a paltry $3.49 million per team. A Designated Player would count for a cap hit of $436,250. The actual salaries versus the cap hit can be wildly different. Kaká made just under $7.17 million, almost twice the salary cap limit, playing for Orlando City in 2016. New York City FC, attempting to buy relevance as the newer of two teams in New York, paid out $5.61 million to David Villa and just over $5.9 million to Andrea Pirlo, the ageless wonder from Italy. That's three times the salary cap for two players. Toronto FC outdoes them all, boasting a trio of Michael Bradley at $6.5 million, Jozy Altidore for $4.825 million and Sebastian Giovinco at more than $7.1 million, for a total of just under $18.5 million spent on three players. That's more than five times the salary cap of Toronto FC on just three players.

The Designated Player Rule has made teams who can afford it into successes. New York City FC, in only its second year in the league, finished second in its conference. It lost to Toronto FC in the playoffs. Toronto carried on after beating New York to defeat the Montreal Impact and came within a shootout of winning the MLS Cup, losing to the Seattle Sounders. Toronto returned the favor, beating Seattle in the 2017 MLS Final. And lest you think Seattle was a scrappy underdog, it won the MLS Cup with

Designated Players Clint Dempsey ($4.6 million) and Nicolás Lodeiro ($1.7 million) leading the way.

So it seems that owners, after imposing a salary cap, have looked for all sorts of ways to move out from under the restrictions they won by shutting down their leagues. Sometimes, owners are less interested in creating the exceptions listed above than in seeing how they can exploit loopholes in the current cap. This was a problem for the NHL after the 2004 lockout, which we'll talk about below.

Notably, Major League Baseball does not have a salary cap. Instead, it has a "Competitive Balance Tax," its version of a luxury tax. In a luxury-tax system, teams that spend over a threshold dollar amount must pay a tax based on the amount they went over. In 2017, the MLB's luxury tax threshold was $195 million. As of the 2016 collective bargaining agreement, teams that go over the threshold for the first time are taxed at a rate of 20 percent of the amount that they were over. And prior to the 2016 collective bargaining agreement, teams that consistently spent over the salary cap paid a higher tax rate — in year two, teams were taxed 30 percent, and in year three and beyond, 50 percent. The 2016 collective bargaining agreement added a surtax for teams that are $20 million above the luxury tax threshold. Even the simplest systems are complicated in sport.

2.7 CAP CIRCUMVENTION

Sometimes exceptions are bargained. Sometimes loopholes are found by enterprising general managers and agents. Or as Gary Bettman said as he prepped for the 2012–13 lockout, "We made, at the time, what we thought was a fair deal. It actually turned out to be more fair than perhaps it should have been."

The way a salary is calculated for salary-cap purposes in the NHL is based not on the particular dollar value of the contract in any given year but on the "Annual Average Value," or AAV. The AAV is calculated by taking the entire value of the contract and dividing it by the number of years of the contract. For example, if a player signs a $25 million for five years, the AAV is $5 million, meaning that the player has a $5 million cap hit for five years. This is the case whether the contract looks like this:

CONTRACT STRUCTURE 1

YEAR	1	2	3	4	5
SALARY	$5 million	$5 million	$5 million	$5 million	$5 million

or like this:

CONTRACT STRUCTURE 2

YEAR	1	2	3	4	5
SALARY	$8 million	$8 million	$4 million	$2.5 million	$2.5 million

A few years into the life of the NHL salary cap, teams began to figure out that the second structure of contract could be beneficial for the teams and the players. Looking to find a way to pay their stars market value but still remain under the salary cap, some teams started to award "front-loaded" or "back-diving" contracts. These contracts would pay a player handsomely in the first years of the contract, but the salary would become worth a lot less in later years by making the contract long-term (over 10 years). Having a lot of low-paying years at the end of the contract could greatly reduce the AAV of the contract, in turn reducing the "cap hit" for the life of the contract. Since the salary cap was expected to rise over time, a lower AAV was expected to give these teams even more room to maneuver under the cap in the future.

The Detroit Red Wings were the leading team in this regard. Henrik Zetterberg signed a 12-year contract beginning in the 2009-10 season. The contract paid him around $7.5 million for the first eight years of the deal before dropping to $7 million in year nine, $3.35 million in year 10, and $1 million per year in years 11 and 12. This contract gave the Red Wings a way to pay Zetterberg about $7.5 million during his most productive years but endure a cap hit of just under $6.1 million. Johan Franzen signed a similar deal that year. For his 11-year contract, Franzen is paid $5 million to $5.5 million for the first seven years, then $3.5 million during his eighth year, $2 million during his ninth year, and $1 million during his final two years. This structure brought his cap hit to just under $4 million per year. While the NHL perhaps privately grumbled about such deals, no action appears to have been taken against them.

Following Detroit's lead, the Vancouver Canucks figured that they should do the same. When it came to extend star goaltender Roberto Luongo's contract, the Canucks signed Luongo to a 12-year, $64 million deal in 2009, to begin in 2010. In this case, the AAV of the contract came to $5.3 million per year. However, the contract was structured so that Luongo was set to earn $10 million in his first year and $6.7 million in the next five years, with the last four years at $3.4 million, $1.6 million, $1.0 million and $1.0 million.

Like other, similarly structured contracts, this meant that Luongo would receive more cash up-front — closer to his market value — and less at the back end of the contract, when he would be less effective and probably a backup goaltender, or would retire. This was a good contract for the team, which maintained a reasonable salary cap hit, and the player, who was now guaranteed more money. However, this deal was altered by the NHL in the fallout of the Ilya Kovalchuk arbitration, which dealt with a similar contract structure.

Less than a year after Luongo signed his pact with the Canucks, Ilya Kovalchuk signed a contract with the New Jersey Devils. This deal was for $102 million over 17 years (2010 to 2027). Like Luongo's contract and the various Red Wing contracts before it, Kovalchuk's was front-loaded, with most of the money paid out in the early years and less at the end. Not only was this the longest contract in NHL history, it would cover Kovalchuk until he was 44 — and in the 20 years prior to the Kovalchuk deal, only six NHL players (out of about 3,400) had played to the age of 42 — with only Chris Chelios playing past 43.

The contract pushed the boundaries of the practice of front-loading contracts. Until this point, front-loaded contracts generally had about two-thirds of the contract at a number somewhere around market value for the player, while the last three or four years saw the salary drop to a number that was perhaps artificially low. The Kovalchuk contract took this practice to an extreme. Here is how the contracts compare:

SEASONS 1–2	SEASONS 3–7	SEASON 8	SEASON 9
$6 million	$11.5 million	$10.5 million	$8.5 million

SEASON 10	SEASON 11	SEASON 12	SEASONS 13–17
$6.5 million	$3.5 million	$0.75 million	$0.55 million

The NHL rejected the Kovalchuk contract, claiming in true lawyer language that it had "intended or has the effect of defeating or Circumventing the provisions of the CBA." The NHL pointed out that 97 percent of the salary was to be paid out in the first 11 years, while the last 3 percent would be paid out over the last six years.

The case went before an arbitrator given the task of interpreting what he called the "cryptic" collective bargaining agreement. The CBA did not place specific limits on length of contracts or on the amounts paid out over the lifetime of a contract. However, it did include the "defeating or Circumventing the provisions" stipulation, so the contract could be struck down. In other words, while the contract did not violate the word of the CBA, it did violate the spirit. The arbitrator questioned whether Kovalchuk would even bother playing the final six seasons, given that it would be about a 95 percent reduction from his previous earnings, and the salary may even have ended up below the mandatory league minimum salary (which was $500,000 per year at the time and is currently set at $750,000 in 2021–22 in the current CBA). As a result of all of this, the arbitrator found that the contract could not stand.

After the ruling, what happened? Kovalchuk renegotiated with the Devils, inking a 15-year, $77 million deal. Three years later, he "retired" from the NHL to go and play in the Kontinental Hockey League, the Russian professional league, where he is playing to this day. The New Jersey Devils were initially fined and lost two draft picks for their actions — a third-round selection in 2011 and a first-round selection that had to be forfeited sometime before 2014. While the third-round selection was forfeited, the Devils asked the NHL to reconsider the penalty. Apparently deciding that the Devils had learned their lesson, the NHL did not require them to forfeit the first-round pick but instead allowed them to pick 30th overall (i.e., at the end of the first round) in the 2014 draft, and reduced the fine.

Perhaps the biggest casualty of the Kovalchuk decision was Luongo and the man who signed him to the contract, Canucks president/GM Mike Gillis. A common worry of lawyers in negotiating contracts is that although you attempt to predict how the parties might bend the rules of the contract, you cannot catch everything. In this case, the Kovalchuk contract led to the NHL and NHLPA negotiating a "cap recapture penalty" in the next collective bargaining agreement. Although it only applied to about 20 contracts in the NHL, like Luongo's.

While front-loaded contracts were meant to pay the player more now, with a lower cap hit in the future, the cap recapture penalty raises the cap hit of players who retire before their contracts are over. In the case of the Vancouver Canucks, if Roberto Luongo retires before his contract ends in 2021, the Canucks would have a significant salary cap hit, reducing their competitiveness. The per-year numbers, as reported by James Mirtle in 2014, are:

| YEAR LUONGO RETIRES | CAP RECAPTURE PENALTY | | PENALTY TERM |
	FOR VANCOUVER	FOR FLORIDA	
2016	$1,420,062	$508,605	6 years
2017	$1,704,075	$886,459	5 years
2018	$2,130,093	$1,453,240	4 years
2019	$2,840,124	$1,287,209	3 years
2020	$4,260,186	$73,147	2 years
2021	$8,520,373	$0	1 year

Although the Canucks wanted to trade Roberto Luongo and move on to Cory Schneider as their goaltender of the future, the changes in the contract rendered Luongo "untradeable." As a result, in June 2013, Schneider was moved to the New Jersey Devils for the ninth overall pick in the 2013 Entry Draft (which the Canucks used to select Bo Horvat), and Luongo looked to remain with the Canucks for years. However, Luongo was not long for the Canucks and was traded to the Florida Panthers in March 2013, along with Steven Anthony, for goaltender Jacob Markstrom and Shawn Matthias — with the Canucks picking up 15 percent of Luongo's salary going forward.

At year's end, Vancouver owner Francesco Aquilini fired Gillis for signing Luongo to a contract that Aquilini had approved and that the NHL itself had initially approved. Such is pro sports.

These loopholes are entirely legal means (unless a ague argues otherwise after the fact) for teams to gain a competitive advantage. However, leagues and owners have engaged in shadier tactics that, to paraphrase the NHL's own language, "intends to or has the effect of defeating or Circumventing the provisions of the CBA" that they negotiated.

2.8 COLLUSION

The other way that owners sought to keep control over salaries was through simple collusion. This was most blatant in baseball in the mid-to-late 1980s. The MLB commissioner at the time was Peter Ueberroth, who had gained prominence for successfully organizing the 1984 Summer Olympic Games in Los Angeles. The L.A. Games are fondly remembered today for achieving the impossible — making a profit. The $250 million made by the L.A. Games, largely through the aggressive recruiting of sponsors — a novelty at the time — made Ueberroth *Time*'s Man of the Year. Shortly before the Games, Ueberroth was selected to be the commissioner of baseball, and he ran baseball the same way he ran the L.A. Olympic Games — with a focus on the bottom line.

Ueberroth told owners that they were fools for spending so much money to win the World Series, and for signing such long-term contracts. The message to owners was: spend less, over shorter terms. In the off-season of 1985, 35 players were free agents, but only four changed teams. Many star players did not even get an offer from another team. The MLB Players Association filed a grievance.

Undeterred, the owners continued their tacti

strong-armed by Ueberroth, in 1986, prompting a second grievance in February 1987. While this was going on, arbitrator Thomas Roberts found that in the off-season of 1985, the owners had violated the CBA by colluding to keep player salaries down. He awarded damages of $10.5 million to players who were affected, and seven of the free agents from 1985 were allowed to offer their services to any team without losing their existing contracts — becoming what was known as "new look" free agents.

The owners kept up their work, establishing an information bank to share data not just about player salaries but about offers being made to players in free agency. The MLBPA filed a third grievance. While this grievance was underway, the second grievance was decided by arbitrator George Nicolau in 1989. Finding that the owners had violated the collective bargaining agreement in 1986, he awarded damages of $38 million and created more "new look" free agents.

Finally, the third grievance was decided, and the arbitrator in that case awarded damages of $64.5 million and ordered owners to compensate players for losses related to the money and bonuses the players would have received had they been able to sign multi-year contracts.

Ueberroth stepped down in early 1989, before the final two arbitration awards were decided. Today, he is credited with making baseball financially solvent, as baseball teams were breaking even or making a profit in 1988, whereas in 1984, most were losing money. However, a lot of that profit was probably undone by a settlement of these collusion cases reached by players and owners in 1990, in which the owners paid the players $280 million.

The NFL owners did something similar in 2010. The NFL's collective bargaining agreement was initially negotiated in 1993 as part of a court settlement and was extended several times. In 2006, it was extended until the 2012 season. However, it gave both the owners and the NFLPA an "opt-out" clause whereby either could shorten the deal by one or two years.

The NFL owners exercised the opt-out in 2008, shortening the agreement by one year, which made the 2010 NFL season an "uncapped" season. The premise behind this clause was that the owners, faced with spiraling salary costs due to an uncapped season, either would not exercise the opt-out or would be incentivized to get a deal done as fast as possible to prevent further uncapped seasons. Remarkably, teams did not compete for the best players and try to drive up salaries. Instead, salaries generally remained flat, as if there had been a cap all along.

The reason why salaries did not rise soon became clear. The NFL had warned teams against increasing their spending. To back up those warnings, in 2012, the NFL fined the Dallas Cowboys and Washington Redskins for overspending on player salaries in that uncapped year. The Cowboys were fined $10 million and the Redskins $36 million for breaking rules that were not even in place during the 2010 season. If you think this sounds like collusion, similar to what baseball saw in the late 1980s, the NFLPA agreed. They filed a lawsuit against the NFL, alleging collusion and damages of $4 billion. Unfortunately for the NFLPA, the federal courts dismissed the suit, based on language in the new collective bargaining agreement that dismissed all prior lawsuits.

2.9 THE ROLE OF THE COMMISSIONER IN ALL OF THIS

To this point, we've talked about some of the league commissioners and the roles they have played in particular incidents. Kenesaw Mountain Landis was the first commissioner of any sport. Other historically significant commissioners include Bowie Kuhn, Pete Rozelle and Peter Ueberroth. But who are these commissioners? Where do they come from? And what do they do?

Commissioners are the CEOs of the leagues. The team owners ultimately run the leagues, and their approval is required for major decisions such as admitting new teams or relocating existing teams. The commissioner, meanwhile, oversees the day-to-day operations. Ultimately, the commissioner's main role is to protect the "integrity of the game," to use the NHL's term, or to act in the "best interests of the game," to use baseball's words. In practice, commissioners have wide-ranging duties. They mete out discipline to players for on-field and off-field misconduct, negotiate television rights agreements, settle disputes between teams, negotiate agreements with other leagues for player transfers and more. Notably, the commissioner acts for the owners during collective bargaining. Therefore, it is the commissioner, with the backing of the owners, who leads the charge and conducts the public-relations push for things like salary caps. With all of these roles, it should be no surprise that three of the five current major-league commissioners were lawyers, with the other two having business backgrounds.

Commissioners are elected by the owners and serve

at the pleasure of the owners. It appears that the owners have been pretty happy with their commissioners for the most part, as being commissioner is often a long-term gig, lasting a decade or more. Among current commissioners, Roger Goodell has been commissioner of the NFL since 2006, Don Garber has led MLS since 1999 and Gary Bettman has overseen the NHL since 1993. Adam Silver ascended to the top job at the NBA in 2014, while Robert Manfred became commissioner of baseball in 2015. The new guys are expected to be in the position for a while, if the terms of their predecessors are anything to go by. Paul Tagliabue was commissioner of the NFL for 16 years, David Stern spent 20 years as the top man of the NBA and Bud Selig, who started off as an "interim" commissioner, lasted 23 years as the head of MLB.

But owners aren't always happy with the commissioners. Baseball commissioner Fay Vincent resigned his position following a no-confidence vote by the owners. The owners were particularly upset over rising player salaries, as well as declining television ratings and the fear that this would lead to less revenue in the future. There were other grievances that pushed their anger over the top and led to Vincent's ouster. However, a commissioner who has the confidence of the owners can withstand an onslaught from fans and players. Gary Bettman has been mercilessly criticized, at times unfairly so, for decisions made by the NHL on everything from southern expansion (Nashville turned out to be a great decision after some growing pains; Atlanta, less so) to television broadcasting deals (the 2-year, $130 million Outdoor Life Network deal? — it turned out better than expected, especially for the network that became known as Versus, and then the NBC Sports Network, which currently pays the NHL almost $200 million per year). On the other side, despite the fans' and NFLPA's anger over the disciplinary procedures (or lack of procedures) used by Roger Goodell, the fact remains that he maintains the confidence of the owners and is likely to remain in his position for a long time after signing a 5-year contract extension worth up to $200 million in December 2017.

Ultimately, the commissioners serve the owners and advocate in the interests of the owners. Sometimes a commissioner will discipline an owner — think of the Ilya Kovalchuk contract. But commissioners need to be careful to not bite the hand that feeds — think of the reduction of punishment for the Kovalchuk contract. So when you think "commissioner," think "owners' representative."

2.10 IF THE CAP DON'T FIT . . .

What does this tour of competition law, labor law and the restraints negotiated by both sides show? It shows how the current structure of sports in North America is a monopoly. Owners and leagues set the rules — but many of them are also collectively bargained with the players' unions.

If the players have a weak union such as the NFLPA, the leagues will be able to impose more restrictions to the salary cap, more severe restrictions on free agency and fewer guarantees on player contracts. However, if the players have a strong union such as the MLBPA, they will have more bargaining power and will be able to strike deals for softer salary caps, better free agency for players and fewer restrictions on free agency — something more resembling baseball's system.

Because the systems are bargained does not mean that the players have simply accepted the restrictions. Keep in mind that, as in many labor negotiations, the employer has more bargaining power than employees. Team owners can absorb greater losses than players, as team owners often have other businesses that they can use to keep themselves afloat. Most players, however, only have their salaries from the team. Some have endorsements, and some can play abroad (at the risk of injuring themselves). But most don't have these options.

The solution — for owners, at least — has been a salary cap negotiated (or imposed in some cases) with players unions.

Leagues and team owners have touted the salary cap as the silver bullet that will ensure their sport greater stability — and so greater profits. This claim is treated as received wisdom by the owners, as though any sport without a salary cap is somehow sub-par and destined for the dustbin of history. NBPA director Michele Roberts said that this reverence for keeping salaries lower is misplaced. "Why don't we have the owners play half the games?" Roberts told *ESPN The Magazine*. "There would be no money if not for the players . . . Let's call it what it is. There. Would. Be. No. Money . . . Thirty more owners can come in, and nothing will change. These guys [the players] go? The game will change. So let's stop pretending."

Owners and league commissioners, however, have

claimed that a salary cap is vital to the survival of their leagues. Following the 2004–05 NHL lockout, commissioner Gary Bettman proclaimed: "Now the team's ability to compete is based upon its hockey, front office and team-building skills, not on the team's ability to pay. We have emerged as partners with our players and our fans." NBA commissioner Adam Silver has shared similar sentiments. "The NBA's success is based on the collective efforts and investment of all the team owners, the thousands of employees at our teams and arenas, and our extraordinarily talented players," Silver stated in 2014. "No single group could accomplish this on its own. Nor is there anything unusual or 'un-American' in a unionized industry to have a collective system for paying employees — in fact, that's the norm."

Players are less gushing about caps, seeing them as a necessary evil. ESPN's Bryan Windhorst reported that LeBron James was jealous when he heard that Detroit Tigers star Miguel Cabrera signed a contract guaranteeing him $292 million over the next 10 years. "I said 'wow,'" James told Windhorst. "I wish we [the NBA] didn't have a salary cap . . . He's the best player in baseball, and the best players in each sport should be rewarded," James added. "It'd be nice to sign a 10-year deal worth $300 million." At the time, James was "constrained" to a $19 million annual salary.

The experience of other professional sports leagues suggests that teams can survive, and even thrive, without a salary cap — as we can see with MLB and its luxury tax, and the pure free-market approach in European soccer leagues that we'll talk about in part 3.

Despite the claims by leagues that salary caps are the only way to keep the teams afloat, fans and players can reasonably question whether the salary caps actually do what they were designed to do. The NBA and MLS have enough exceptions to their salary caps that it's questionable whether the caps serve as true caps at all. Meanwhile, "cost certainty" has not prevented teams from claiming they still lose money — as they habitually do upon the expiry of every collective agreement. Nor has it prevented teams from shutting down operations, like several teams have in MLS, or outright claiming bankruptcy, like the NHL's Phoenix Coyotes did in 2009.

Overall, it seems that the salary cap does not quite live up to its lofty promises. What it does accomplish is to restrict the salaries of players such as Russell Wilson, Steph Curry and Connor McDavid — and these players are the reason fans turn up to games and buy cable and streaming packages for leagues. However, the salary cap is only the latest example of the strategies that teams and leagues have used to restrict players. Free agency and the draft have been around much longer, to the point that they have somehow simply become accepted as "part of the game."

As we've mentioned, soccer has maintained a pay-for-play model that captures a global following, creating dynamic properties. Even here in North America, fans know Ronaldo and Messi, Barca and Man U. The salary cap, by comparison, spreads talent thinly across too many teams, reducing the game to a defensive struggle as coaches seek to protect their jobs.

What would happen if the salary cap simply disappeared? As we show in part 3 of this book, players would get paid their market value. Some poorly run or marginal markets that couldn't afford to pay for top-end players would have to compete at a lower level to let the stars shine at the top. As when Hollywood eliminated vaudeville in many small cities, and as water finds a level, the same would happen to sports.

PART 3
BRINGING BACK
REAL COMPETITION

There is a joke that goes: How many Torontonians does it take to screw in a light bulb? One. They just hold the bulb while the world turns around them. Toronto has a complex. What's theirs is theirs. What's yours is theirs, too. So long as it's not a sports championship. Toronto has been starved for trophies (other than the CFL's Grey Cup) for decades. The Blue Jays followed up their two World Series championships in 1992 and '93 by spending 22 years out of the playoffs. The Toronto Maple Leafs have infamously avoided getting anywhere near a Stanley Cup victory since Canada's Centennial, 1967, when there were only six teams in the NHL. The NBA's Raptors remain trophyless, currently playing under the shadow of LeBron James.

But even those who chafe beneath the yoke of the Big Smoke had to like what they saw in the 2017 MLS Finals. On an unseasonably warm November afternoon, Toronto FC did everything right in its championship rematch against the Seattle Sounders. A series of new household names wearing the red of Toronto FC — Jozy Altidore, Michael Bradley, Sebastian Giovinco, all brought in off the free market — was established on this day beside Lake Ontario. The crowd of 30,584 chanted, threw toilet paper rolls and sang their hearts out.

Just like that, Toronto had its first league championship outside of the CFL in decades. (One helpful announcer expunged the Argos entirely and said the last Toronto championship was the Blue Jays World Series triumph in 1993.) The match was watched by 2.4 million fans in North America, with 1.3 million Canadians watching Toronto hoist the Cup. The match the year before was even bigger, setting records for MLS Cup viewership, with 3.5 million North Americans turning in to see Seattle defeat Toronto in a shootout. Watching either game on TV, you couldn't help but notice that they were everything that the 2016 Grey Cup game, held in the same stadium, was not. The soccer fans were unruly, obnoxious, passionate and wholly authentic.

The disappointment when Toronto FC lost to Seattle in 2016, and the elation when TFC got its revenge, was genuine. The Grey Cup attendees, except for some traveling Ottawa RedBlack fans, had all the excitement of a crowd milling around the vehicle-registry office. Even with more fans watching the Grey Cup on TV — about 3.9 million viewers — the greater excitement for the sport of soccer was palpable. It might be because Toronto was the host team in the MLS Final, while the Grey Cup was between Ottawa and Calgary. But the difference remains.

Now, Toronto does have a weakness for the shiny object. Whatever was hot in Los Angeles last month is now *en vogue* in Toronto. So TFC could just be the latest infatuation. After years of truly bad TFC teams, average attendance jumped from 18,000 in 2012 and 2013 to over 22,000 from 2014 onwards. It looks like Toronto may be on to something when it comes to soccer. In our endless desire to be entertained to death, soccer might now have moved up from an afterthought to second or third billing on the card. Certainly the popularity of MLS teams in Vancouver and Montreal echo Toronto's success. Why?

Well, as everyone who knows a striker from a corner kick has noted, Canadian kids have played the game in impressive numbers for decades. You can't go by a park in the springtime without seeing hundreds of little gamins pinwheeling around the field while their parents scream like lunatics. That is, until they're teenagers and move on to more domestic stuff, like hockey or basketball. The great conundrum for Canadian soccer has been how to translate all these child participants into grownup participants playing for Canada at a World Cup. Until that chilly night by Lake Ontario, that is.

It's more than simple coincidence that the Argos are sputtering at the gate while TFC packs the compact stadium by Lake Ontario. While TFC has been attracting over 22,000 fans per game since 2014, the Argos brought in an average of 17,000 in 2014, 12,000 in 2015, 16,000 in 2016 and 13,900 in 2017. Put simply, the CFL is being overtaken in southern Ontario by soccer. The crowd has moved on. The Double Blue can take comfort in knowing they're not alone. Research from ESPN shows that soccer is surpassing almost every sport in North America (except football) in the 12-to-24 age group. With Latino Americans, it's number one.

A sport that 20 years ago was considered an ethnic pastime, about as cool as wide lapels and paisley ties, is now the thing to do if you're a young person. The formation of Major League Soccer and the cool of David Beckham, Lionel Messi and Cristiano Ronaldo coming through on their tablets and phones have made soccer hip with a young demographic. Also spreading the magic dust on soccer in Canada and the United States is the popularity of the women's game in the Olympics and the World Cup, now carried in prime time by eager networks. Stars such as Christine Sinclair and Abby Wambach have attracted a generation of young women to the sport. No wonder 52 percent of fans for MLS are aged 18 to 34 — the highest such percentage of any team sport in North America.

What can soccer teach the CFL and those other sports about attracting the coveted young cohort? Participation numbers and a North American league alone don't explain it. The romance of the "beautiful game" isn't the big hook either.

Soccer is soaring because it understands that the sports industry has changed. It is not a regional or even a national business anymore. The sport has pushed to maximize its reach as a worldwide entertainment vehicle. While globalization is under attack in other realms, going past your borders is still cool in pro sports. Knowing that international stars such as Ibrahimovic, Messi and Rooney sell its product worldwide, soccer has increased its outreach via television and digital sources. North America now has more live soccer on TV than the rest of the planet. Fans who aren't crazy about MLS can sample live broadcasts of the greatest club and national teams in Europe, South America and Asia.

The jerseys and logos of the teams are hot sellers online. Kids want Sebastian Giovinco's FC jerseys or Paul Pogba's kit from Man U instead of the sweater of the CFL's MVP (in 2017, it was Mike Reilly of Edmonton, in case you were wondering). Or they'll wear the jersey of Brazil's Neymar instead of a Sidney Crosby Penguins sweater. Young people who've been playing the sport from an early age are transitioning into fans of the sport as they watch soccer at any time of day on cable and over streaming services.

The NHL? It can't get organized enough to participate in the 2018 Olympic hockey tournament — the most visible aspect of its sport in the world. How does that sell your sport?

3.1 REWARDING SUCCESS, NOT FAILURE

In North America, the best teams get a chance to enter a playoff system where "anything can happen." As often as not, the best team in a league's regular season is not lifting the championship trophy at the end. The most that the best team over a 16-game, 82-game or 162-game season gets is home-field advantage in series, which — depending on the sport — may have negligible value. While the play-offs make the end of a season more exciting, they hardly reward sustained excellence. Meanwhile, the worst teams get the best chances to obtain the top young talent.

In European soccer, the league championship is awarded to the top team at the end of the season. Each team plays each other twice (home-and-away), and the team with the best record wins the championship. No seeding, no cross-overs, no forced divisional rivalries. Just competition. While this format may cause situations where the top team is decided a month in advance, which can be a little anticlimactic, often the quest for the championship comes down to the last couple of games of the season. If that weren't enough, in the top leagues, there is more on the line than just the championship. The top teams in "lower" leagues get the chance to earn a promotion to a higher league. While others in the Premier League must fight to the last game to avoid costly relegation.

Meanwhile, the best of the best get a chance to participate in international competitions. Soccer has graduated from the regional model for its franchises to an international model through events like the various "Champions Leagues" for club teams, and the UEFA Euro Championship and FIFA World Cup for national teams. These competitions have become spectacles that captivate Europe, Asia and North America's top markets and generally provide some sort of soccer competition year-round.

Both promotion to a higher league and playing in the European competitions are financial boons for a team. For example, Hull City is a team that has regularly bounced between the English Football League Championship (England's second-tier league) and the Premier League (the top tier) in recent years. When it was promoted to the Premier League in 2013, the team went from receiving about $2.75 million per year from the Championship's TV deals and other income to $85 million from the Premier League equivalent.

Participating in the UEFA Champions League can be lucrative for teams as well. In 2016–17, the 32 teams that participated in the group stage received about $13.8 million each and another $1.6 million for each win and just over $0.5 million for each draw. The winning team took home another $16.8 million. In the secondary European competition, the UEFA Europa League, participants received $230,000 just for coming out, and the victors received just over $7 million.

On the other side of the ledger, teams that do poorly are not rewarded but are faced with real consequences. Teams that finish at the bottom of a league are relegated to a lower league. When teams are relegated, they are able to play teams that should be at about their same level, but they also lose money as a result of playing in a less popular lower-tier league.

Teams that are relegated don't lose out entirely, however. In the English leagues, for example, teams receive "parachute payments" that are meant to ease the shock of relegation. If a team had players who commanded Premier League salaries lost over $80 million in income after relegation, it could go bankrupt quickly. Parachute payments, often in the tens of millions of dollars, tapering off over three years, give teams time to adjust and an incentive to get promoted again.

These real costs place importance on who finishes at or near the bottom of the league at the end of the season. In the Premier League, the teams from 18th to 20th place are relegated to the EFL Championship. As a result, the "relegation fights," which determine who gets to remain in the top leagues and who will drop down, are must-watch soccer. Millions were rapt as Leicester City engaged in a relegation fight in 2014–15 known as "the Great Escape." In 2014, Leicester was promoted to the Premier League for the first time in 10 seasons. After 29 games, Leicester had only four wins and was at the bottom of the 20-team Premier League. In North America, this situation would lead a team to tank for a draft pick. In the Premier League, it meant that Leicester seemed destined for relegation. So Leicester fought. In its final nine games, it racked up seven wins and one draw to finish 14th, well safe from relegation. The result was tense soccer matches with a lot on the line.

Following the Great Escape, the *Daily Mail* newspaper wrote that the hope for Leicester's next season was to "spend a little more time off the bottom of the table and build on this stunning finish to the season. A more relaxing ride all round probably." Instead, Leicester picked up where they left off, going on a year-long Cinderella run to win the Premier League, capturing a global audience in doing so. The thing is, it's hard to tell which was more exciting in the moment: the unexpected championship win or the relegation fight of the year before. It's certainly a far cry from an NHL or NBA team tanking to get a draft pick.

Despite the staggering financial success of this model, the legacy sports in North America don't seem particularly interested in this formula so far. They're too busy shutting down their sport through labor disputes. Too preoccupied fiddling with salary caps so they can keep 30-plus team leagues trundling along to notice that the earth has moved beneath them. With global outreach, there's no need to station a franchise in every corner of the continent, as the leagues did from the 1960s onward. And it appears that the franchise model and its attendant props of salary caps and parity are being rejected by younger fans.

You can see how North American leagues might be reluctant to recognize the change. With its enormous gambling following, the NFL has felt a smug confidence that allows it to resist change, despite CTE concerns, Colin Kaepernick's kneel-down fight with President Donald Trump and countless penalty flags delivering seismic blows to the NFL and its TV ratings. The other sports, with their bloated inventories of meaningless regular-season games, are on shakier ground. The NBA's 12-man rosters give the league star power.

But they, too, are losing support among younger fans, says ESPN. Perhaps no sport is more vulnerable than the NHL. Saddled with its reliance on postseason revenues, the NHL lives in a straitjacket it created decades ago to sell to medium and small markets in North America. In spreading its teams across 31 American cities instead of concentrating its focus and players in, say, 20 cities, it's missing out on creating the international TV footprint that soccer is enjoying.

Again, salary caps are a symptom of the problem. Limiting spending and creating mediocre teams as a form of false parity is an attempt to mask the underlying problem of too many teams, too many players and too much game inventory that means little. It stems from an obsession with the outdated concept of parity.

3.2 IT'S MY PARITY AND I'LL CRY IF I WANT TO

Exactly when did the North American sports population decide they wanted parity over excellence? Whether it was planned or just happened, parity is the animating principle of the pro sports industry and has been since the 1960s, when teams like the Boston Celtics could win seven straight NBA titles. Or when the Montreal Canadiens gathered a constellation of stars that would win 15 Stanley Cups between 1955 and 1979. As some experienced sports followers call it, "the good old days."

Those days are gone. To see NHL commissioner Gary Bettman rhapsodize about 12 teams fighting for the final six playoff spots is to see a man enter the seventh stage of bliss. He's not alone. NBA commissioner Adam Silver, NFL commissioner Roger Goodell and MLB commissioner Rob Manfred go into similar hyperventilation about their concocted pennant or playoff races, too. As if close means entertaining.

Close can mean games where coaching systems — honed by hours of video study — triumph over talent. In the current 31-team NHL, even the worst club has a few skilled players. You can't ask slugs to produce like stars. To protect against this skill gap, coaches have reduced the game to a contest of systems. Or, to be precise, a contest to see who can execute the same systems better. The immediate success of the expansion Vegas Golden Knights in 2017–18 shows how an enterprising general manager can take players from a relatively open market (through the expansion draft), make smart decisions on how to build a team of complementary players, without waiting for a draft pick, and succeed to an extraordinary level in the NHL.

But that's not enough to win the big prize. At one point, the NHL was a league of contrasts. Teams had identities: the Flying Frenchmen of Montreal versus the blue-collar Toronto Maple Leafs; the Big Bad Bruins of Bobby Orr and Phil Esposito versus Bobby Hull's dynamic Chicago Black Hawks. It was a contest of styles that transcended simply rooting for the crest. With six or even 12 teams, there was room to let players improvise and create a new dynamic as they played.

For today's fan, it's a contest to see which team executes the standard system better. Statistics geeks will tell you there are differences between teams, but ask even a devoted fan to tell you the difference between Montreal's system and Toronto's system, and you'll get a blank look. Video analysis becomes more important to winning than letting a player's inner muse emerge. Every once in a while, a skilled player will poke his head above the fray with a brilliant move. But just as quickly, the coaches will devise a way to drag him back to the rigid systems. The top is kept firmly on the box.

Tell a young NFL fan that the quarterback once called the plays, and his head will explode. Or that catchers called all the pitches. Or that NBA stars worked out the best plays for themselves on the court. Or that one coach, not three, stood behind the bench at an NHL game — without a telex in his ear from a fourth coach in the press box. They probably won't believe you.

It's hard to blame coaches. If your job depended on winning, you'd want to minimize the chances for mistakes, too. But if, because the owners have decided to distribute talent over too many teams, you can't concentrate great players on a team the way Barcelona or Arsenal or AC Milan does, then you have to make do with what you have. Bring the skilled players down to the level of the role players and guard against the second guess from fans and media. Play a system that reduces mistakes, not one that emphasizes creativity. Stay close to the conventional. Hew to what everyone else is doing. Avoid criticism.

In other words, maintain parity.

The word *parity* is the pretty dress they use to hide the homely baby: the franchise business model leagues have been rocking since the LBJ administration. Put simply, the leagues sought to exploit the 1960s revolution in televised sports by placing franchises across the continent where they might best cash in on the regional and national TV sports craze. Sell hockey like it was a McDonald's franchise. Find new sources of revenue besides game-day income. In the 1960s, 60 percent of an NFL franchise's value came from ticket sales, but even then, everyone could see that there were new pots of gold in broadcasting. So leagues expanded to the largest television markets, regardless of the product they put out. Why is there an NHL team in Phoenix? Because, as of 2017, Phoenix is the 12th-largest TV market in the U.S. Even the NFL, with the largest broadcast revenues, can't escape this logic. The NFL signed television deals worth billions of dollars with national networks, all without a team in the second-largest television market — Los Angeles. Now that L.A. has two NFL teams again, will that boost the league's bottom line or the quality of the games? It's hard to say yet, but it's unlikely. TV, digital streaming from anywhere — that's the future.

As leagues expanded, the money came flooding in for owners, through expansion fees, TV rights deals and merchandising money. In 1969, *U.S. News* wondered about the bursting of the sports bubble, as NFL team values went from $1 million in the 1950s to $10–16 million in the late 1960s. Even commissioner Pete Rozelle was quoted as saying, "The future of pro football certainly is healthy. I wouldn't say that the boom is over. But we can hardly continue to grow at the same percentage rate as we have in the past." The report expressed concern about the addition of *Monday Night Football*, about stadiums that were at capacities in the 70- to 80-percent range, and whether the market was simply saturated.

The alarm was unwarranted. TV contracts grew from CBS offering $4.65 million for the NFL in 1961 to a range of TV networks paying over $6 billion to cover the league today. Merchandising went from a small sideline run by teams to a multi-billion-dollar operation coordinated by the league's head office.

As a result, the equity value of teams has skyrocketed. The current NHL has 31 teams, the NFL 32, the NBA and

MLB 30 each. The annual *Forbes* report on the equity in pro sports teams is the bible of pro sports (even as leagues faux-protest the numbers contained therein). The L.A. Clippers were bought by Donald Sterling for $12 million in 1981. Despite decades of dismal performance, and the NBA essentially forcing Sterling to sell the team, the Clippers still managed to fetch $2 billion in 2014. That's a rate of return of 16.7 percent per year — much better than the stock market. The NFL Carolina Panthers went on sale in the winter of 2017–18 and Owner Jerry Richardson, selling the club over allegations of sexual improprieties, collected $2.5 billion from new owner David Tepper on a team he'd acquired for $200 million in 1993. Even accounting for inflation, that's a tidy return. Having paid in the hundreds of millions for the right to field a team (in the case of the NFL, billions of dollars), owners have a lot of skin in the game of keeping the fans engaged. That means seeing their team be successful.

But for owners more interested in just the bottom line, and those who want to win, the leagues need something more, lest the owners leave en masse, devaluing all those multi-million-dollar franchises. To keep those owners in the game, leagues had to develop a way to engineer a weighted competition that drags the best down to the middle and vaults the worst up to mediocre status. Thus, the dreaded P-word. Parity. You may only have one championship trophy, but you can give a lot more teams a whiff of success through endless postseason series and spreading talent as thinly as possible across the rosters of the league. With the aid of a compliant media, you can sell the whole jumble as caviar.

As we showed in part 2, parity has been produced by torturing monopoly laws and asking the hired help to take less than it might get in an open market. Over the decades, legal Whac-A-Mole — the game of keeping 30-plus owners happy by defying market value for players — has resulted in brutish labor lockouts, silly strikes and exasperated fans who just want their sports.

In locking out their players, owners promised fans reasonable ticket prices, franchise stability and stars staying close to the home they had when they entered the league. It's been a poor bargain for fans. Look at ticket prices: the best ticket to Super Bowl I was $25; the average ticket to a regular-season NFL game in 2016 was $92.98. Coming out of the NHL's 2004–05 lockout, the average ticket price was $43.13. By 2016, it was $62.18. Tickets to high-profile events such as a Super Bowl or a Game 7 in the NBA or NHL can soar into the tens of thousands (all prices courtesy of statista.com).

Because of this ticket-price escalation and the improvement in broadcast and television quality, many people today experience sports not live but via TV, tablet or phone. Similarly, "free" TV coverage of games has morphed into subscription-based cable networks or league-owned packages of games that can cost hundreds of dollars a year. So while owners have canceled months — sometimes entire seasons — in the quest to defy the market for payrolls, the benefit has not extended to the fans.

Another justification for the lockouts was franchise stability. How has this worked out? What we can say is that owners believe in free agency for themselves. This free agency is exemplified by the movement of franchises

— even longstanding franchises dating back half a century — to a market that is seemingly greener. As in, green with Abe Lincolns and Ben Franklins. In the 1990s, four NFL teams and four NHL teams moved to greener pastures. Since 2000, the NHL saw the Atlanta Thrashers move to Winnipeg, and the NBA had three teams relocate: Vancouver to Memphis, Charlotte to New Orleans, and Seattle to Oklahoma City. Most recently, the NFL saw its St. Louis Rams move back to Los Angeles in 2016 and the San Diego Chargers move to Los Angeles in 2017, while the Oakland Raiders will move to Las Vegas in 2019. Strangely, the league without a salary cap, MLB, saw only one franchise move — the Montreal Expos to Washington (via Puerto Rico) in 2005.

While pro sports owners moan about the need for restraints on player movement from team to team, they have less compunction about an owner backing up the moving vans when his attempts to secure funding for a free stadium from the local government are not rewarded. Moves from L.A. to St. Louis and back to L.A. were motivated by the presence or absence of stadium financing from the city of St. Louis. The NFL's St. Louis Cardinals absconded to Phoenix and a cozy deal in the desert when they weren't able to get a financial embrace from their former city. Longtime Cleveland owner Art Modell made the switch to Baltimore when his stadium demands went unheeded in Cleveland but received a better hearing in Maryland. Cleveland recanted its fiscal prudence, built a new stadium and received an expansion team, to be called the Browns once again. And the pace of this free agency has only picked up as leagues turn the screws tighter on their salary caps. Even the *Madden* NFL video game has a franchise relocation option for players.

At the heart of this brinksmanship is the billionaire owners' insatiable desire for easy access to public funds. Somewhere along the way, their need for a new stadium or arena became conflated with the needs of a community or state or province. Despite all of the research showing that massive investment in sports stadiums is a net loser for cities, mayors and governors seemingly can't resist the urge to lavish public money on these private businesses. And when they do resist — as the city of Calgary did with the Flames' new arena proposal in 2017 — NHL commissioner Gary Bettman suggested that the team would move if the demands for public money weren't accepted.

Leagues boast about the intangible returns to a city being known for its baseball, football or hockey team — although there are few economic studies that back up such fever dreams. But the cities know that if they don't play ball with the teams, the moving vans will come — in the middle of night if needed, as when the Baltimore Colts fled to Indianapolis to avoid a pending court order keeping the team in place.

3.3 A SYSTEM YOU CAN BET ON

It's no secret that a big part of sports' popularity today is based on gambling. This is almost ironic, given that historically, gambling has been related to scandal in sports. The Chicago Black Sox scandal, in which some players intentionally lost the 1919 World Series in exchange for money from gamblers, shook baseball to its core. One outcome of that incident was the appointment of former judge Kenesaw Mountain Landis as baseball's first commissioner. He cracked down by banning the offending Chicago players for life from MLB. Baseball, of course, has seen other gambling scandals since then, including Pete Rose's lifetime ban for betting on baseball games. More recently, Tim Donaghy, an NBA referee, was banned from the NBA for tipping off bettors to games that he and other refs officiated. He was eventually sentenced to prison for his actions.

While gambling or match-fixing by players and officials is justifiably seen as something to be stopped, gambling by fans is a boon for sport. Fans bet on any and every aspect of sport. Final standings, game winners, point spreads, spot bets and fantasy sports are just some of the major forms of sports gambling. Adam Silver, commissioner of the NBA, estimated in 2014 that some $400 billion is wagered on sports every single year. It also breaks down traditional team loyalties as bettors wager on other teams and players rather than the heroes of their home team.

The amount spent on gambling is somewhat strange, because the United States, adhering to its puritan roots, has largely outlawed gambling on sports (in Canada, sports gambling is operated by the provincial governments). The *Professional and Amateur Sports Protection Act*, or PASPA, was enacted by the U.S. Congress in 1992, at the urging of professional sports leagues and the NCAA. PASPA prohibits gambling on amateur or professional sports. A "grandfather" clause allows sports gambling to continue in Nevada, with some limited gambling in Delaware, Montana and Oregon.

Seeking to revitalize the casinos of Atlantic City, New Jersey has challenged PASPA as an infringement on states' rights and therefore a violation of the U.S. Constitution. This argument was rejected by the courts in 2013. Delaware has also challenged the statute, but with the same luck as New Jersey. However, New Jersey's 2017 appeal to the Supreme Court was approved by a 6–3 vote. States can legalize sports betting, opening an enormous new source of revenue for governments and, ironically, sports leagues. Throughout the lawsuits, the major sports leagues and the NCAA have sided against the states, trying to keep PASPA in place.

But the leagues are not a monolith anymore on the subject of betting. Adam Silver, who made a splash in his first major test as NBA commissioner by banning racist L.A. Clippers owner Donald Sterling from the league, showed that he was not going to support the status quo under PASPA. In November 2014, Silver penned an op-ed in the *New York Times,* acknowledging that gambling on sports is not going to go away. What to do about it? Silver suggested that "sports betting should be brought out of the underground and into the sunlight where it can be appropriately monitored and regulated." He called on Congress to adopt a modern framework to regulate gambling on sports, and to provide the oversight to protect sports, and to protect gamblers.

The NHL has dipped its toes in with the Golden Knights team in Vegas. Fans can bet throughout the game on the sport. The NFL has also announced that it will place the Oakland Raiders in Las Vegas in 2019. Sports gambling in North America is no longer a black-market operation. Another incursion has been the appearance of daily "fantasy sports" wagering games online. Fantasy baseball and fantasy football have been around for decades, with fantasy baseball beginning in the 1950s and fantasy football in the 1960s. However, it was in the late 1970s that fantasy sports began to become mainstream, with baseball's "rotisserie" leagues and football's "Coach the Pros" league. While fantasy sports have largely been limited to local leagues, among friends or co-workers (like in the TV show *The League*), the internet has caused fantasy leagues like DraftKings to explode. Players around the world can play against each other in fantasy leagues, and there is clearly money to be made.

Fantasy sports reached dizzying heights in the mid-2010s. Ads for DraftKings and FanDuel were everywhere. These companies were engaged in "daily fantasy sports." In normal fantasy sports leagues, participants choose their players and are stuck with the roster for the season unless they trade, like a real team. But daily fantasy sports participants choose new players for any given day. The appeal is obvious: why wait a season to see if you've won money when you can play every single day? Daily fantasy sports companies claimed that players could win millions of dollars by simply picking the best-performing players on any given day. Now that's incentive to follow sports more closely.

Daily fantasy sports companies have been embroiled in controversy since their rise to prominence. Attorneys general from a number of U.S. states have declared that daily fantasy sports is gambling and in violation of PASPA. There have also been allegations of "insider trading," with employees from each company participating in competitions put on by the other company — and getting rich as a result. Despite the controversies, media companies backed the daily fantasy sports companies. Bewilderingly, MLB, the NBA and the owners of the Dallas Cowboys (Jerry Jones) and the New England Patriots (Robert Kraft) were also backers of DraftKings and FanDuel. So on the one hand, leagues and teams complained to courts about the evils of gambling to convince the courts to uphold PASPA, while on the other hand, they fund companies that are engaged in what can only be called gambling on sports.

Sports teams' greater acceptance of gambling (at least tacitly), has probably made expansion to Las Vegas easier. One of the concerns about leagues having teams in Las Vegas was that local fans would bet on the teams, perhaps tainting the purity of sport; another was that players would get into all sorts of trouble there. However, the NBA and NHL have frequently hosted their awards shows in Vegas, without much incident. In 2016, the NHL took the first step by announcing an expansion team in Las Vegas. The NHL's stamp of approval did not come cheap, with billionaire owner Bill Foley paying $500 million to the league.

Enforcing parity is in theory married to gambling. Parity, at least in theory, ensures that any outcome remains unpredictable, which is better for gambling. But with point-spread gambling and fantasy sports, parity is not required, as it doesn't matter who wins or loses; it matters how they play the game. One thing gambling does do for sports is generate interest in a product that has been watered down by the leagues' push for mediocrity. Who is going to watch a Thursday Night Football game between two basement-dwelling teams in November? Someone who has a quarterback or receiver selected in his daily fantasy football league would. Loyalties are breaking down as a result.

But is this the best the leagues can do?

3.4 LEVELING THE PLAYING FIELD BY RESTRICTING FREE AGENCY

Restrictions on free agency were meant to prevent the specter of all the best players bolting to either New York or Los Angeles or forming some sort of super-teams. The "nightmare" was something like the Miami Heat, where LeBron James and Chris Bosh joined Dwayne Wade in 2010. The Heat made it to the NBA Finals in four straight years, winning two championships. Or today's Golden State Warriors, who in 2016 added superstar Kevin Durant in free agency to a team that had already been to two straight NBA Finals at the time — with Durant getting a ring in 2017.

Yes, free agency played a role in those teams. But most excellent teams are not necessarily created by gathering top free agents. The Boston Celtics put together their "Big Three" through the draft (Paul Pierce) and trades (Kevin Garnett and Ray Allen). Rajon Rondo, crucial to the Celtics' success of the late 2000s, was also drafted. The San Antonio Spurs, a model of consistency since the early

1990s, drafted both of their big names — David Robinson and Tim Duncan — and traded for their heir apparent, Kawhi Leonard, on the night he was drafted. Manu Ginobili and Tony Parker were also drafted. In other ways, there is more than one way to build a champion, even in the era of free agency.

Meanwhile, some super-teams just don't work out. In 2012–13, the Los Angeles Lakers looked to continue a run of recent strong seasons. That summer, they traded for two-time NBA MVP point guard Steve Nash and three-time NBA Defensive Player of the Year center Dwight Howard, who joined Kobe Bryant and a team that had won back-to-back championships in 2009 and '10. The Lakers looked set. However, only five games into the season, after a 1–4 start, the team fired its coach. The Lakers finished at 45–37, just sneaking into the playoffs, only to be beaten in four straight games by the Spurs. That was the last playoff run for the Lakers for a while; in the years since, the Lakers have been at the bottom of their conference.

You'll probably notice that a lot of the focus above is on basketball teams. That's because a major free-agent signing or two can dramatically alter a basketball team. With just seven or eight players playing most of the time, a team can afford to run a "Big Three" and spend little on support, and still have a puncher's chance at winning a championship. However, this setup doesn't work as well with the other sports. A few key free agents might push an otherwise good team to greatness, but there must be some underlying strength to the team already. And even if the stars are signed, it doesn't always work out.

Remember the 2003–04 Colorado Avalanche? It's okay if you don't. Just before the season began, the team signed Paul Kariya and Teemu Selanne. Kariya and Selanne had been stars for the Ducks, but Selanne had since been traded to the San Jose Sharks. The pair took discount deals to play in Colorado, with Kariya signing for $1.2 million (down from the $10 million he had earned with Anaheim, which he had just led to the seventh game of the Stanley Cup Finals), while Selanne signed a $5.8 million deal (turning down a $6.5 million option from the Sharks). For a total of $7 million, the Avalanche added two of the NHL's best players to a team that already had Peter Forsberg and Joe Sakic. Both players had, by their standards, forgettable seasons, Kariya with 11 goals and 36 points in 51 games, and Selanne with 16 goals and 32 points in 78 games.

The team finished second in the division and petered out in the second round of the playoffs, losing to the San Jose Sharks. After the 2004 lockout, Kariya went to the Nashville Predators for two years at $9 million, where he rediscovered his offensive touch, notching 31 goals and 85 points in his first year there. Selanne, meanwhile, signed a one-year, $1 million contract and went on to score 40 goals and 90 points in 2005–06 — winning a Stanley Cup in 2007, and remaining a Duck until 2014. Why did the Selanne/Kariya experiment not work? It might have had to do with the retirement of legendary goaltender Patrick Roy the year prior.

These examples suggest that super-teams are probably not all they are cracked up to be, and in many cases, are not even feasible. For every "Big Three" on the Miami

Heat or Boston Celtics, there's a failed experiment like the Los Angeles Lakers or the Colorado Avalanche. And in the salary-cap era, teams cannot even put together a super-team unless all of the players take far less than market salaries, for the sole purpose of winning a championship.

Another stated goal of salary caps is to force the best teams with the most progressive management to shed their advantages by trading or selling off players when the cap fits too tightly. The Chicago Blackhawks are a great example, as they head into a third overhaul of the players around their winning core. Since their first Stanley Cup this decade, they've had to dump a virtual All-Star team: Dustin Byfuglien, Brian Campbell, Troy Brouwer, Andrew Ladd, Dave Bolland, Michael Frolik, Nick Leddy, Brandon Saad, Patrick Sharp, Johnny Oduya and Teuvo Teravainen. And still they've won three Cups even as the cap system conspires against them.

The parity argument that a salary cap will "level the playing field" suggests that fans do not want to watch a league in which teams can win by outspending each other. Of course, there are differences in salaries spent by teams — the range between the floor and the cap — but this should be less pronounced than in non-capped leagues. The end result is that poor teams will be able to compete with rich teams. But how does parity play out in a capped league versus the relatively free-market MLB?

From 2000 to 2017, 20 different MLB teams played in the World Series, with 12 unique World Series champions. During that time, the NFL had 17 different teams play in the Super Bowl, with nine unique Super Bowl champions; the NHL had 19 teams play in the Stanley Cup Finals, with 10 unique Stanley Cup champions; and the NBA had only 13 teams play in the NBA Finals, with only eight unique champions.

PARITY OF FINALS APPEARANCES/ CHAMPIONSHIPS (2000–2017)

LEAGUE	NUMBER OF SEASONS	NUMBER OF TEAMS WITH AT LEAST ONE FINALS APPEARANCE	NUMBER OF TEAMS WITH AT LEAST ONE CHAMPIONSHIP
MLB	18	20	12
NHL	17	19	10
NFL	17	17	9
NBA	18	13	8

Speaking of the NBA, the playoffs themselves are often dismal affairs for most of the matchups. Every now and then, there will be an intriguing first-round matchup. But the playoffs are usually a march of mediocre teams playing to be beaten by either the Golden State Warriors or the San Antonio Spurs in the West, and whoever LeBron James is playing for in the East (and if you think that's a joke, consider that a James-led team has made eight straight NBA Finals from 2011 to 2018). It seems like the final matchup is almost a foregone conclusion. And if you think it's competitive, consider the routes the Golden State Warriors and the Cleveland Cavaliers took to three straight NBA Finals series from 2015 to 2017. In nine conference series, the Warriors swept four and went to seven games just once. Cleveland cut through the East's "best" like a hot knife through butter, with six sweeps in nine series and none going over six games. Now, we are proponents of excellent teams, so we're not saying whether this is a good thing or a bad thing. But one thing we are certain of: it's not parity.

All of these results might seem odd at first glance, particularly since the teams that can make the MLB playoffs are limited to 10, including Wild Card teams (and only eight before 2012), while the NFL allows 12 teams to make its playoffs, and the NBA and NHL have 16-team playoff brackets. Yet even with its limited playoff spots, in the five seasons from 2012–2016, 21 of MLB's 30 teams (or 70 percent) made the playoffs (including the wild-card play-in).

What is the point of the playoffs if not to give all teams that make it a chance of "upsetting" a higher seed and advancing to the finals? In the late 2000s, some executives of an MLB team spoke to a class at Harvard Law School. They said their goal was not actually a championship every year — that's essentially asking the impossible. Their actual goal was making the playoffs, ideally with home-field advantage. After that, they felt that the playoffs were a bit of a crapshoot. And that seems to be the ideal of the playoffs, an anything-can-happen environment in which a Cinderella team can make a surprising run at a championship with a bit of good luck and a lot of hard work. But if that's not the case, as it seems in the NBA, then why have the playoffs at all?

Whether one looks at playoff participation, the competitiveness of the playoffs or the diversity of champions, it seems that MLB has more parity than other leagues do — and all without a salary cap.

3.5 THERE'S A DRAFT IN HERE: THE AMATEUR DRAFT DOESN'T LEVEL COMPETITION

While a variety of teams are sharing in the championships (although it's much more competitive in the less forgiving environment of Major League Baseball), the picture at the bottom of the standings is less impressive. Many teams have come to the conclusion that there is no benefit to spinning their wheels in the middle of the standings, hovering on the "bubble" of getting into the playoffs and likely getting soundly defeated by the top seed or missing the playoffs. Because of the amateur draft process, teams in this "middle" get no shot at the franchise players and also lose out on postseason revenues. Understanding their plight, they now resort to tanking — losing on purpose to get the best young players entering the league.

That was the conclusion of the MLB Houston Astros owners earlier this decade. After a series of disappointing years, they decided to gut the team, sell their stars and build a homegrown champion. Starting in 2012, they lost 106, 111, 109 then 92 games in a season. By 2015 they'd accumulated a number of top prospects on friendly contracts. Added to veterans such as Justin Verlander — acquired by trade — the Astros won the 2017 World Series. The lesson has not been lost on other MLB owners and those in other leagues. The draft system is the most economical means to winning a title, even if it means a lot of losing to get there.

The current draft system, devised by team owners, not only punishes teams that manage to do well but rewards mediocrity. In extreme cases, outright ineptitude and incompetence are virtues. Nowhere is this more apparent than in manipulation of the entry draft through the "tanking" exhibited by the Astros. By losing more games over a season, a team finishes lower in the standings, which leads to a higher draft pick. The team can hope to "win" in the long run by "losing" now.

As we've already discussed, the entry draft is supposed to serve as a leveler for teams. Those teams who finish at the bottom of the league get the rights to the top incoming talent, which should make them better. Like many systems, it works in theory, but the reality shows us something else.

With fewer superstars than teams, and with young players paid a lot less than veterans, the importance of getting a franchise draft pick on a reasonable contract outstrips the need to win in the present. Teams unlikely to make the playoffs (a determination usually made around the trade deadline) get less competitive by dumping good players for draft picks. So if you are a fan of a team that looks like it will make the playoffs, then you get to watch a competitive team. But if you are a fan of a team that is unlikely to make the playoffs, you may be subjected to some pretty awful games.

Tanking reached its logical extreme from 2013 to 2016, during the tenure of Sam Hinkie as general manager of the Philadelphia 76ers. Hinkie, who has an MBA from Stanford University and worked with Bain Capital before becoming the GM of the 76ers, is best known for engaging in what is derided as "the Process."

Prior to Hinkie's arrival, the 76ers were a "bubble" playoff team, finishing seventh, eighth and ninth in the conference in the previous three seasons and upsetting the Chicago Bulls in the 2012 playoffs. Upon taking over the team, Hinkie decided that the best way to move from mediocrity to competitiveness would be to strip the team down and rebuild through the draft. This thinking is fairly standard, particularly in basketball, where one player can make a significant difference — as shown by Michael Jordan, LeBron James and others.

The difference between simply rebuilding through the draft and "the Process" was the timeline. While teams that seek to earn a top pick perhaps have a single "down" season, "the Process" had a longer timeline. Hinkie went to work, trading away good players and players with bad contracts for draft picks. In the 2013–14 season, the 76ers finished with a record of 19–63, good enough for second-last in the NBA.

With the Cleveland Cavaliers winning the draft lottery, the 76ers had the third overall pick and used it to draft Joel Embiid. The concern with Embiid was that he had undergone surgery that looked to keep him from playing basketball for six months. He eventually missed both the 2014–15 and the 2015–16 seasons. That summer, the 76ers also traded for Dario Saric, who was playing in Europe and only joined the team for the 2016–17 season.

These moves did not help the 76ers, who lost one more game than the year prior, going 18–64 and finishing third last in the league in 2014–15, ahead of only the hapless Minnesota Timberwolves and the dysfunctional New York Knicks. Picking third in that year's draft, the 76ers selected Jahlil Okafor. On their opening night for the 2015–16 season, the 76ers had five rookies on the roster and no players over the age of 24; not surprisingly, this youthful squad finished last with a record of 10–72.

In 2016, Hinkie resigned as GM of the 76ers. As of this writing in late 2017, however, Hinkle's bet looks poised to succeed. Okafor has been traded to New Jersey, but Embiid, still plagued by injury, is a dominating presence on court when he plays. Other top picks such as Ben Simmons are recognized as franchise players. Critics agree they are a probable playoff team in 2018 and on the way to a superior squad. But in an Eastern Conference where a .500 record gets a team into the playoffs, which is where the 76ers have been most of the season, let's not equate "success" with "excellence."

"The Process" is based on the hope that continually drafting high for several years will lead to long-term success. The common examples mentioned are the Pittsburgh Penguins' drafting Marc-André Fleury with the first pick in the 2003 NHL Entry Draft, Evgeni Malkin with the second overall pick in 2004 and Sidney Crosby with the first pick in 2005. These three players were integral to Pittsburgh's future success and their Stanley Cup championships in 2009, 2016 and 2017 (although Fleury admittedly had a diminished role in winning the last two Cups). The same can be said for the Chicago Blackhawks' drafting Jonathan Toews third overall in 2006 and Patrick Kane first overall in 2007, and winning Stanley Cups in 2010, 2013 and 2015. Looking to basketball, the immediate impact of LeBron James on the Cleveland Cavaliers after being selected first overall in the 2003 NBA Draft cannot be overstated.

But the Edmonton Oilers have shown the short-sightedness of simply drafting at the top of the pile. After making the Stanley Cup Finals in 2006, the Oilers looked to be the symbol of the salary-cap era in the NHL — a small-market team that could manage the cap and remain just as competitive as the big-market teams. The Oilers quickly imploded following the departure of Chris Pronger, finishing in the league's basement for 10 seasons, including two straight seasons as the league's worst team. They received three straight number one draft picks during this time, drafting Taylor Hall in 2010, Ryan Nugent-Hopkins in 2011 and Nail Yakupov in 2012.

It's possible that the Oilers tanked in one or several of these years. However, it seems just as likely that they were simply ineptly managed. Rotating through coaches on an almost annual basis (seven coaches in eight seasons) and recruiting their management from the Glory Days of the 1980s Oilers, the team lacked direction. And the three draft picks? Only Nugent-Hopkins remains with the team; Hall and Yakupov were sent out of town in 2016 — Hall as part of a trade to obtain a much-needed defenseman in Adam Larsson, and Yakupov for spare parts.

However, the saga did not end there, as the Oilers won the lottery one more time in 2015. They received the gift of Connor McDavid, who won the Art Ross Trophy as the highest-scoring player in only his second year in the league. The Oilers made the playoffs in 2017 and looked to be credible contenders for the Stanley Cup with a few more additions. However, the Oilers crashed out of the playoffs again in 2018, and their future seems anything but certain. Showing that getting generation players like

McDavid is no guarantee of success. A consistent management and development system might be more important.

A lingering problem that the Oilers face is their inability to draft well in the later rounds. It takes no creativity to draft the surefire talents. However, outside of the first few players, the draft appears to be a crapshoot. First-overall players can be central components of a championship team — see LeBron James or Sidney Crosby. But there are also busts that toil in near-obscurity for their careers — see Andrea Bargnani or perhaps Nail Yakupov.

Meanwhile, numerous players drafted in the later rounds have highly productive careers. The Detroit Red Wings famously drafted Pavel Datsyuk 171st overall in 1998 and Henrik Zetterberg 210th overall in 1999. Although some pundits touted the "Detroit model" of finding value in later draft picks, it does not hold water: if this was a "model" that was replicable, why would Detroit not draft these players earlier in the draft, instead of running the risk that they would be picked up by other teams? It's more likely that Detroit got lucky with these draft picks. It is perhaps better to look at draft picks as lottery tickets — maybe you hit it big, but maybe you don't. Bill Belichick of the New England Patriots has earned plaudits for trading high draft picks for a number of lower draft picks — in effect using one lottery ticket to buy a bunch more lottery tickets. In sum, the draft is no surefire way to establish competitive balance, as teams with the top picks may never improve, while teams that are excellent seem to remain so, despite drafting later on.

3.6 ATTEMPTS TO REBALANCE THE DRAFT

Purposefully mediocre lineups and the stripping of assets are hallmarks of tanking. Hinkie's "Process" appears to have been to tank for a few years, draft the best players possible, and then rise to the top. However, "the Process" was so blatant that even the NBA put forward a proposal to change the entry draft to prevent tanking teams from benefiting with high draft picks. NBA commissioner Adam Silver himself said that "I think there's an unfair pressure on some of our teams to under-perform because there becomes this view in those markets that they're better off performing poorly in order to win over the long term."

The draft has already been tinkered with to reduce tanking and to avoid subjecting fans to uncompetitive and unentertaining games. The main tool has been the draft lottery. The draft lottery takes teams that qualify for the top picks of the entry draft and places them into a lottery for the top pick. The number of teams has changed across leagues and over time, ranging from only the absolute worst teams to all the teams that have not made the playoffs. In the NHL, there also used to be a limit to how many spots teams could move up in the lottery, but now, as in the NBA, any team that finished out of the playoffs has a chance to move up to pick in the top three. The lottery gives each team a "weight" based on its finish, with the worst teams having a higher weight — meaning they have a higher chance of winning the lottery. In theory, this reduces the incentives for teams to tank, as they will only gain a small advantage by finishing last.

It happens that teams who finish last and allegedly

tanked still not do receive the number one overall draft pick. In the 2006–07 NBA season, the Memphis Grizzlies and Boston Celtics respectively finished worst and second-worst in the NBA. The top two draft picks that year were Kevin Durant and Greg Oden, with experts projecting that either of them would be a franchise savior. However, following the draft lottery, the Portland Trail Blazers and the Seattle SuperSonics won the top two picks, with Memphis picking fourth and Boston picking fifth. Portland drafted Greg Oden, who saw limited time on the floor during an injury-riddled career, while Seattle saw success with Kevin Durant — but in an Oklahoma City Thunder uniform, as the SuperSonics relocated the next season.

During the 2014–15 NHL season, the Buffalo Sabres and Arizona Coyotes engaged in a "race to the bottom," with many media outlets openly wondering if the teams were tanking to get the best shot at McDavid. The plan worked out for neither team, as the Edmonton Oilers infamously won the draft lottery, and the right to select McDavid.

While not tanking, the Vancouver Canucks were facing a rebuilding year in 2016. *USA Today* predicted that the Vancouver Canucks would finish the upcoming season with 65 points. Meanwhile, Electronic Arts, the company that makes the NHL video games, predicted that the Canucks would finish with only 63 points, which would put the Canucks among the decade's worst teams — the Toronto Maple Leafs of 2015–16, in finishing last in the NHL, still managed 69 points. "Impossible," stated team captain Henrik Sedin. The local newspapers rallied around their boys in blue and green. The *Vancouver Sun* dismissed the predictions, saying the Canucks would be an 83-point team. The *Vancouver Courier* suggested that the Canucks would "hang around the playoff picture." The website CanucksArmy was more ambivalent, saying that "they might not be a 65 point team, but they're probably not a playoff team either."

In this case, the local optimists were a little right. The Canucks started off with four straight wins, bringing ecstasy to Vancouver. This was soon tempered with nine straight losses. In the end, Vancouver did not finish with 65 points. It beat that mark by four, reaching 69. This wasn't good enough for last in the league, as the Colorado Avalanche proved hilariously inept at the game of hockey, getting 48 points. While that wasn't the worst record of all time, in the era of parity, a team shouldn't be finishing 21 points (or 10.5 wins) behind the second-worst team.

And what did the Canucks get for beating the "expectations" of *USA Today* and EA by four or six measly points? Instead of picking at number two in the 2017 NHL Draft, they picked at number five. That's because three other teams won the draft and skipped ahead of the Canucks and Avalanche. Dallas moved from number eight to five. Philadelphia, within striking distance of the playoffs, moved up 11 spots, from 13 to two. And New Jersey jumped from five to one. The real loser in this system was the Las Vegas Golden Knights, who were hoping to pick third to begin to build their expansion team. But in the lottery, Vegas fell to number six.

Even with the lottery, there is still incentive to tank, to increase a team's odds of winning the lottery. For the odd times that a team moves up several spots in the draft lottery to be able to draft a franchise-defining talent, many more drafts come and go with the absolute worst teams keeping their right to draft the absolute best young talent.

A modest proposal for reform was considered by the NBA in 2014, whereby the top six choices, not the top three choices, could be determined by the draft lottery. That meant a team that finished last could draft as low as seventh. This reform was too radical for teams like the Sixers, and although it was supported 17–13, approval required 75 percent support from the owners, and the teams engaged in tanking obtained just enough support to defeat the proposal.

Another reform, proposed by Boston Celtics Assistant GM and general counsel Mike Zarren, is being considered by the NBA. Zarren, a product of Harvard Law School, literally invented, and then reinvented, the Wheel. The Wheel would have teams rotate through each draft slot (1 to 30) over a 30-year period. Some concerns were raised by owners: a team that benefited from a top draft choice might spend the next years low in the draft order; the league would be locked into the system for 30 years. Another concern was that the top young prospects could time their entry into the draft to join a better team or a desired market. And giving top prospects choice simply wouldn't do.

Zarren has since proposed that teams get placed into groups of three or six, and those groups rotate. For example, the Chicago Bulls could be in the group that picks in the 1-to-6 slot one year, the 25-to-30 slot the next year, the 19-to-24 slot in year three, 13-to-18 in year four and 7-to-12 in year five. Every six years, any given team would have one of the top six picks. That would require better draft asset management, and as the Sixers have shown, having consecutive years of top draft pick does not a better team make.

3.7 MOVING BEYOND THE DRAFT

Given the problem of tanking, why not just eliminate the draft altogether? You might worry about how teams will allocate players if there's no draft. There are two alternatives already in use: the college system and the European system.

College football and basketball teams do not have a draft but instead convince the hundreds of thousands of high school players to attend a particular college — often, in some small markets, far from the urban center. While some colleges have advantages over others — a winning program, geographic placement, educational reputation — recruits are likely to choose colleges for a variety of reasons. Playing time — exposure to pro scouts — is a key. So is a high-profile coach. And national TV exposure matters, too. Yes, there are corrupt practices and shady deals, but no more than occur in the systems leading to the pro ranks in other sports.

Then there is the European approach. European soccer teams have academies — training programs where the top professional teams are responsible for training the next generation of players. Academies provide training, and sometimes education and housing, to young players. Teams scout local players, sometimes as young as seven years old, and invite them to join their academies.

Academies are important to soccer teams as a cheap way of identifying and training top players. On average, top-flight teams spend about $0.5 million to $1.5 million per year on their academies. Compared to the tens of millions of dollars a team could spend on the transfer market in any given year, the academies are a cost-sensible way of raising the best talent. Not all academies seek to train players to play on the top team, however. Some academies hope to train good players and then sell them on the transfer market. Either way, teams are incentivized to have good academies.

Nowhere has this system been stronger than in Germany. After a disastrous showing at the UEFA Euro 2000 football tournament, where Germany had two losses and a draw, finishing at the bottom of its group, the German soccer federation decided that something had to change. The biggest change was the requirement that every team in the top two divisions of German soccer operate youth academies. The results cannot be denied — the German national team has made it to the semifinals or finals of the 2008, 2012 and 2016 UEFA Euro tournaments and the finals or semifinals of the 2002, 2006 and 2010 FIFA World Cup before winning it all in 2014, largely with a core of young players. Even the professional teams have benefited from the German focus on youth training, with the top German teams relying mostly on German talent as opposed to spending millions on the transfer market. Even the professional teams benefited, with the 2013 UEFA Champions League final contested between Bayern Munich and Borussia Dortmund in an all-German final.

Academies place the burden of training on teams and force them to have some skin in the game. This is completely different from the North American system, where training is left either to junior leagues or to colleges. How many times have you heard that a quarterback, despite playing for four years at the college level, is not "NFL-ready"? Why is there such a large disconnect between the college game and the NFL? If NFL teams were required to train players, maybe the players would be better prepared for the NFL style of play. And maybe the teams would be a little less reluctant to cut players at whim, having invested time and money into training them.

Academies would also be good for the players. Right now, there's no incentive for colleges and junior leagues to care about the long-term health of players. The priority for those programs is to ensure that players get drafted. They'll only have the player for a few years, so who cares what the long-term effects are? But if a team is required to train a player for a decade or two, maybe it will care a bit more about the long-term health and development of the players.

3.8 TOO BEAT TO COMPETE: HOW SALARY CAPS DUMB DOWN PLAY

The law of unintended consequences has enjoyed a field day under the cap as owners and their lawyers engineer ever-more complicated Larry Bird clauses and back-diving contract language to prevent superstars from hitting the market, which we talked about in part 2. But other unintended consequences have come about. The need for parity and for teams to at least appear competitive, regardless of the reality, has placed pressure on two groups that have had no role in negotiating the current system of sports: referees and coaches. It has also made injuries to star players more impactful than ever.

With talent stretched through the league, the difference between winning and losing on a given night is more and more reliant on a penalty call, a missed strike or a controversial flag for pass interference. With so much riding on human decisions, leagues have had to resort to video replay to get the calls correct and protect the integrity of their product (no small matter when betting floats the boat of the NFL and NBA).

This leads to newspapers like the *Boston Globe* asking: "In close games, how often do NBA referees get it right?" The article says that "as part of a transparency initiative, the NBA began releasing its 'Last Two Minutes' officiating reports to the public on March 2. The reports contain reviews of plays that occur in the final two minutes of regulation or overtime of close games." Or this article on the *Pride of Detroit* blog: "Three ways the NFL can limit the officials' impact on the game: With officiating becoming an increasingly impactful part of the game, we offer three rule changes to improve the NFL and their refs." Then there's this article from *USA Today*: "The NFL admits refs missed 16 game-changing calls in the Jaguars-Packers game."

The effect of this intense scrutiny of referees has been to delegitimize game results. Where once a Guy Lafleur goal or a Tony Dorsett touchdown was proof of the superiority of the players and their teams, every play today is endlessly dissected by officials, television crews and fans.

When winning is always just one call away, litigating decisions helps fans rationalize that their team didn't lose, they simply were robbed by bad calls. Some think this is a reason to do away with video replay and challenges. But the real culprit is the suppression of excellence, which creates so many more close games and crucial calls.

Complicating matters is the gutting of the "middle class" of players. Teams are frequently becoming a mix of high-priced, top-performing veterans mixed with young players whose salaries are constrained by rookie wage scales. The depth that once helped alleviate these situations has disappeared as salary caps crush the middle-class veteran in favor of the cheaper rookies. Look at rosters and wonder where the savvy 30-year-old player has gone? He's gone the way of the dodo as owners look for cheaper help. As such, the caliber of play is subordinated to fitting under the salary cap. With predictable results.

In 2016, a report by Kevin Clark on the Ringer Podcast Network found that the NFL is definitely getting younger, with 25 players younger than 21 playing in the 2015 season, double the 2012 number. NFL teams now stock up on young talent with cost-controlled contracts and splurge on a few veterans. If players don't become stars by the time their first contract is up, they are likely to find themselves out of football altogether. Teams no longer develop players, instead opting to replace the veteran with younger talent. As a result, players no longer have time to develop and learn the system, making the coaches' job harder as they have to reteach their system to incoming players year over year.

So coaches have become conservative, adjusting their schemes to the lowest common denominator. Tactics devolve to dump-and-chase and the "trap" in hockey, intentional fouling in basketball and football coaches ordering field goals on fourth-and-inches. Better to lose by a small amount than take a risk, it seems. In a league that attempts to enforce parity, risks are not rewarded, nor are they tolerated.

With the talent spread thin, the impact of injuries is enormous. Injuries have always played a role in winning or losing games and series. But if your margin for winning depends on the tenuous health of just one or two players, an ACL tear or Tommy John surgery can ruin a team's season. Because all players are tied to rosters during the season, with very few free agents, there are few options for teams beset by injury except to trade for a replacement, robbing Peter to pay Paul.

3.9 INNOVATE OR DIE: UNLESS YOU HAVE A CAP

One of the biggest innovations in sports in the past two decades that hasn't involved a lockout is "Moneyball." *Moneyball: The Art of Winning an Unfair Game,* written by Michael Lewis, was published in 2003 and turned into a movie starring Brad Pitt in 2011. A movie essentially about contract negotiations and spreadsheet analysis may not sound like a blockbuster, but *Moneyball* made more than $110 million at the box office. What was so interesting?

Moneyball represented a radical departure from the past, necessitated by open competition. The Oakland

Athletics had just lost to the New York Yankees in the 2001 playoffs. The Yankees had spent $109 million on their payroll, while Oakland had spent less than a third of that, with just under $34 million. To make matters worse, the A's lost their top two players in free agency to the Yankees and the other $109 million team, the Boston Red Sox. Realizing that they couldn't compete on money, the A's had to find undervalued players, look at different ways of measuring players and seek inefficiencies in the market.

The A's looked for cheap players, not always young, who had the skills that could get them on base. Whether these batters drew walks or hit for singles, the A's figured out that getting on base, and not getting out, was what baseball was all about. No need to overpay someone who will strike out as often as they will hit a home run. Better to pay someone much less who will get on base, keep the game going and defeat opponents by dribs and drabs as opposed to dingers.

As they say, necessity is the mother of invention — and in baseball, without the enforced parity of a salary cap, the A's had to innovate. But they were ridiculed by many in baseball for relying on stats, as opposed to the eyes of scouts. Yet the Moneyball process kept the A's more competitive than they otherwise would have been for more than a decade after they adopted the approach. Once other teams, such as the Boston Red Sox, assumed a Moneyball mindset, the game of baseball changed. General managers could not ignore the changing tide and had to become smarter, expanding their minds and their front offices to include stats-minded individuals. As a result of rich teams emulating their process, the barebones A's lost any advantage they had. They have bounced between winning the pennant in 2012 and 2013, and being a bottom dweller in a bad ball park from 2015–17.

Other leagues have been slower to embrace the Moneyball approach. Some observers wonder whether it's just a case of owners and general managers stuck in the "old ways," and that's likely part of it, but there's also the way leagues are structured. Why should a team bother spending time and resources to innovate if it's almost guaranteed a playoff spot so long as it finishes above .500? Why should teams bother to innovate if salaries are cost-controlled?

That Sam Hinkie's "Process" is considered innovative by anybody shows how little innovation there is in a salary-capped league. Instead of figuring out new ways to scout and evaluate players or improve their performance, managers have spent time trying to figure out how to circumvent the salary cap or improve their draft position. As the salary cap restricts competition, it also eliminates any incentive to innovate. So if you want to see more innovative teams, your best bet is to allow for more competition.

3.10 THEN THERE'S SOCCER: THE BENEFITS TO A NON-SALARY-CAPPED LEAGUE

For owners, players and even fans, it is difficult to imagine a different system than the one we have, because we often think *that's just the way it's always been*, or *this has to be the best way*. This book has given lie to the first claim; we have shown how owners have claimed that they need all of the restrictions to "make the game better" but in fact have adopted them just to improve their bottom line. As for the second claim, we only need to look across the Atlantic at a different system, and the successes and failures that have befallen the owners, players and fans over there.

If you ask the average European on the street, the North American model of sport is strange. They frequently remark that for a hyper-capitalist country like the United States, the professional sports leagues are deeply socialist. Revenue is shared among teams, and pay is capped. The worst teams are awarded with more resources (i.e., draft picks) based on the idea that the best teams and worst teams should not be too different in quality. Training of young players is left to others — junior leagues and colleges that maintain that their players are "student-athletes" (stretching the meaning of *student* as far as it can go, especially in light of the National Labor Relations Board stating in a 2017 memo that the athletes were effectively employees).

Even the best professional teams aren't rewarded with more than the championship and a small payout. The NHL splits $13 million across the teams that make the playoffs: the Stanley Cup champions are awarded $3.75 million (or about $150,000 per player), while teams that make the playoffs receive $250,000 each (or about $10,000 per player). Compared to the $13.8 million a European soccer team can make for simply showing up in the Champions League, these rewards begin to look a little paltry for the grueling months spent chasing the Stanley Cup. And it begins to look more like a Soviet-style organization than a real business.

Meanwhile, Europe, that bastion of social democracies, has a hyper-capitalist sport structure. Teams get to spend what they make. The best teams are rewarded with promotion to higher leagues or participation in championship leagues, which makes those teams even more money. The worst teams sink to lower leagues through relegation. Teams are responsible for their own development and training of players. And players have more freedom to join the best teams and make more money than they do in North America. In Europe, teams "eat what they kill," and the free market generally rules.

One of the justifications for parity is that fans wouldn't stand for a few elite teams dominating their sport through their market power. They cite the dynasties of the Yankees, the Celtics, the Canadiens and others as being "bad" for sports. How does the magnificence of the New England Patriots hurt the NFL? Has it cost the league on its broadcasting contracts? Likewise, has the recent success of the Chicago Blackhawks or (before them) the Detroit Red Wings hurt the NHL? How about the San Antonio Spurs and their sustained excellence over the past two decades? How have they suppressed interest in the NBA?

In fact, it helps a league when there's a benchmark team against which to measure success. For fans, seeing their team matched against the best is a litmus test of excellence. It marks the progress their team is making. But the salary cap produces a flood of games in which evenly matched teams play games decided by referees, injuries or bad bounces. There is satisfaction in rooting for the team's crest, but rarely the satisfaction anymore of knowing you beat the best — especially in the postseason.

But there are examples of how parity is less important than ever — especially at the national or global level. What might life look like in a league without a salary cap?

Funny you should ask, because there is a ready example out there that we've discussed a few times already. Soccer — at least, soccer as it's played everywhere but in North America — goes full commando, salary-wise. There are recent restrictions placed on teams that require teams to keep their spending to the same amount as their revenue — to "break even." But so long as teams can bring in the money, they can spend it as they see it. Just don't go bankrupt like Portsmouth and the Glasgow Rangers did in the early 2010s.

Otherwise, the owners of the top soccer teams in Europe are largely unbound by restrictions and unafraid of greatness. As Gordon Gekko said in *Wall Street*, "Greed is good" when it comes to buying and selling the talent needed to become a cup winner in national leagues or the super-leagues created by UEFA. This means that players such as Lionel Messi are compensated appropriately and won't have to leave their teams as a result of being "cap casualties."

Instead of parsing the legal nuances of the Supreme Court (okay, so there are some decisions by the European Court of Justice, and the odd European Commission ruling — but it's not *ad nauseam*), soccer executives operate in a (largely) free market for talent where teams play at the level they can afford. Teams are then assigned to the level of competition they can best support from the revenues they earn. So England has the ultra-rich Premiership (the most expensive league in the world), the EFL Championship, League One and League Two. Instead of failure being rewarded at the bottom of the table, teams are relegated and promoted. Instead of top young talent being awarded to the laggards in the league, prospects are sold up the food chain until they, and their paychecks, reach the top levels of the sport.

At the elite level, a transfer system allows for the open movement of players twice per year. While the transfer system is sometimes as opaque as the Mississippi, the simple version is that when Team A wants a player on Team B, the sides discuss a transfer fee that would allow Team A to buy the contract. Team A gets a top player, and Team B gets money that it can spend on other players, or on developing its own young players in its academies. Once the player is sold, his contract is torn up and a new salary is negotiated. So transferring not only benefits teams but can also benefit players.

For the top players, these transfer fees can run to stupefying amounts. Recent years have seen Cristiano Ronaldo bought by Real Madrid from Manchester United for £80 million. Paul Pogba moved from Juventus to Manchester United for £89.3 million in 2016. Luis Suarez, on suspension after biting a player in the 2014 FIFA World Cup, was sold by Liverpool to Barcelona for £65 million. And in 2017, Neymar moved on from Barcelona to Paris Saint-Germain for £198 million.

Unlike in North America, players can also emancipate themselves from their contracts — although the system has many wrinkles to be worked out. Player contracts may contain clauses that allow players to buy themselves out of their contracts, and if the contracts do not contain these clauses, the FIFA regulations that govern soccer allow players to do so. However, players are incentivized to stay with their teams and honor their contracts for at least a few years, as the FIFA regulations state that a player may be suspended from playing for four to six months if he buys out his contract within two or three years of signing it. In practice, the buyout provision has proven difficult to implement, with the Court of Arbitration for Sport giving wildly different awards to teams as compensation. But it's a system that, in theory, gives some control to players to get away from teams that don't value them or that might be ineptly managed.

While this system may seem foreign to the North American model, it is, in fact, the way pro sports operated before owners began using amateur drafts and salary caps to divide up the available talent and establish cost control. As baseball stats guru Bill James explained in his 1987 essay "Revolution," "By the early 1920s, every minor-league team was required by the rules of organized baseball to sell its best players to the major leagues. As part of the deal, major league baseball agreed not to sign players straight out of high school. That way each minor league team had its own territory and could sign the players coming out of high school, and make a profit by selling them up the line."

Soccer maintains this food chain to this day, with players being sold up the chain to the top by lower-ranked teams or by players emerging from training centers (often sponsored by teams in the elite divisions). It's accepted that top clubs like Barcelona, Manchester United and Bayern Munich can use their financial clout to assemble great teams. If fans mind, it hasn't shown itself in attendance, TV ratings or merchandise sales. In fact, the excitement around transfers and signings only whets the appetites of the media and fans.

3.11 DOES PARITY PAY?

Now, here is the elephant in the room: the argument that there is not enough parity in European soccer, as the top teams tend to win most of the titles and remain the top teams. The Premier League has been won by one of Arsenal, Manchester United, Manchester City and Chelsea since its first season in 1992–93, with the exceptions of Blackburn in 1995 and Leicester in 2016. Spain's La Liga has generally been home to the Real Madrid–Barcelona arms race, while Italy's Serie A has been won by Juventus, Milan or Internazionale since 2001. And while France's Ligue 1 had a string of four different champions between 2009 and 2012, 2002 to 2008 was all Lyon, and 2013 to 2016 marks Paris Saint-Germain's reign. The Bundesliga has been dominated by Bayern Munich since 1999, but Dortmund, Bremen, Stuttgart and Wolfsburg have also taken home hardware at the end of the season.

So it looks like there might be less parity in the European leagues, as least as far as measuring champions goes. But it's not that far off the enforced "parity" of the North American leagues, which are not as equal as they'd like you to believe, anyways. And, as mentioned before, in Europe, it's not just about winning the championship but also about participating in the Europe-wide leagues, which take in the top teams in the top leagues.

Some skeptics might express concern that fans won't tune in and broadcasters won't pay for leagues that don't enforce parity. But because soccer does not operate on a franchise model, there's never been an incentive to create parity. People accept that the big dogs have to eat and that everyone else feeds on the leftovers. How has this gone over? TV contracts for soccer's World Cup, the UEFA European championship and the various first divisions of top leagues are enormous. In 2015, the Premier League sold its domestic broadcasting rights for £1.712 billion (about $2.23 billion) per season for three seasons. Outdoing itself, it sold its global broadcasting rights for the same three seasons for £2.8 billion (about $3.65 billion) per season. The Bundesliga sold its domestic rights in 2016 for €1.16 billion (about $1.3 billion) per season; La Liga sold its for €883 million (about $989 million) per season, and Ligue 1 did the same for €726 million (about $813 million). Finally, Serie A sold its domestic television rights for three seasons for €940 million (about $1.05 billion) per season and its international rights for €186 million (about $208 million) per season, an amount which some commentators called "disappointing."

Compare these contracts to the North American leagues. The NFL comes out the strongest, selling its television rights for $4.95 billion per season (excepting some money from the league's Thursday Night Football broadcasts on Twitter and Facebook). The NBA signed a TV deal that will see the league receive $2.6 billion per year for its rights until 2025. In 2013, the NHL signed a "landmark" deal for Canadian television rights in which the Rogers broadcasting network bought 12 years of the NHL for CDN$5.232 billion. This only amounts to CDN$460 million per season — not much for a hockey-mad country like Canada. And this is still more than the NHL's $200-million-per-season contract with NBC for the American rights. There are also local deals that add to the revenues of the NHL, but in an American market of 320 million potential viewers, these results are a little underwhelming. Regardless, soccer has certainly proven just as valuable, if not more valuable, a property as North American sports.

And even closer to home, the NCAA football and basketball leagues refute the idea that fans will turn away from sports unless their own team is winning or if the same teams seem to dominate annually. The ranks of the most successful football teams contains the same names almost every year. Ohio State, Michigan, Alabama, Florida State, USC, Oregon, Oklahoma — all have storied programs and have been in the top 20 rankings almost continuously for much of the past decades. In 2010, ESPN agreed to a 12-year deal at approximately $5.64 billion, about $470 million annually, just for the rights to the annual bowl season.

The same goes for NCAA men's basketball. North Carolina, Duke, Kansas, Michigan State, UCLA, Indiana, Villanova — they too are constant powers on the hoops scene. But the popularity of March Madness keeps rising. In 2010, the NCAA signed a 14-year, $10.8-billion contract with CBS and Turner Broadcasting to televise the basketball tournament. On top of that are separate national and regional conference TV deals.

From all its sports, the Southeastern Conference (SEC) made the following in 2017: $476 million total — $34 million per member school; $112 million from bowl games; $17 million from the NCAA Tournament; $347 million from TV deals. Ratings for some of the shoulder bowl games may be tepid, but the College Football Bowl Championship and March Madness remain consistent ratings winners.

The conclusion: fans, and broadcasters, are willing to pay for excellence.

3.12 WHAT ABOUT SOCCER'S CORRUPTION?

Anyone who has paid any attention to soccer in the past decade knows of the rampant corruption at the highest echelons of the sport. On a pleasant day in Zurich, Switzerland, in May 2015, FIFA members gathered for their annual confab and to rubber-stamp a fifth term for president Sepp Blatter. What they didn't know was that Swiss authorities were lying in wait. The police swooped into the Baur au Lac hotel, arresting seven FIFA officials on corruption charges. The U.S. announced that it was cooperating with Swiss authorities in a full-scale investigation into FIFA, with two officials found guilty of racketeering and wire fraud conspiracy in 2017.

Blatter, who had helmed FIFA since 1998, was undeterred, standing for and winning his fifth term as president. He vowed to reform FIFA "starting tomorrow." However, any reforms would be modest. Seemingly oblivious to the fact that he had been in his position for the better part of two decades, Blatter told the FIFA members, "I find the time I've spend at FIFA is very short and it will remain short." He was right on the second part. Only a few days later, he stepped down. After an internal FIFA investigation, he was banned from football activities for eight years — eventually reduced to six by the Court of Arbitration for Sport. Also caught up in the scandal was UEFA president Michel Platini, who was similarly banned.

The corruption under investigation largely involves money being moved around over international television rights. But other actions by FIFA reek of corruption. The selection of Qatar as the host of the 2022 FIFA World Cup? A country of 2.2 million people (just less than the population of Metro Vancouver), with no significant soccer history? And the 105-degree summers? Up against the U.S. and Australia? It doesn't add up.

Leagues are not immune from corruption, either. In late 2016, there were allegations that Premier League managers were taking money under the table for player transfers. In 2015, there were accusations that referees in La Liga were told to "favor Real Madrid" during a match with Barcelona.

But let's not pretend that there is no corruption in North American sport. We've talked about Tim Donaghy, and there are claims that various playoff series have been fixed by leagues (the 1993 Toronto–L.A. series in the NHL, and the 2002 Sacramento–L.A. series in the NBA come to mind) or that the draft lottery has been fixed (the biggest target of conspiracy theorists being the 1985 NBA lottery, in which the Knicks won first pick, allowing them to select Patrick Ewing).

Some may worry that following soccer's lead would bring not just the good (competition) but also the bad (corruption). But most of the corruption in soccer seems to happen at the international level, where there is more opportunity to engage in it and more ways to launder money. A soccer-like system at the North American level, if properly monitored, should not make corruption any more likely than it is under the current system. While there may be more room for shenanigans in the event of transfers, where money changes hands for players, a transfer system identical to the one in Europe doesn't need to be in play. Perhaps a transfer/trade hybrid like the MLS system would be a good middle ground.

3.13 OKAY, SMART GUYS, WHAT WOULD WORK BETTER?

Glad you asked. We'll use the NHL as an example. First things first: we'll give the owners their greatest wish and expand the NHL to 48 teams. You might be thinking *but you said there were too many teams*. There are — at the highest level. But when the NHL reaches 48 teams, we can divide it into two tiers. Let's take the English designations and call them the Premier Conference and the Championship Conference, for now.

We'll then redivide the conferences into two divisions. Again, it doesn't matter what we call them for now, but let's use the names of some of hockey's greats.

Here's what the Premier Conference would look like:

ORR DIVISION

Boston
Buffalo
Miami (Florida)
Montreal
New Jersey
New York (Long Island)
New York (Manhattan)
Philadelphia
Pittsburgh
Tampa
Toronto
Washington

GRETZKY DIVISION

Anaheim
Calgary
Chicago
Dallas
Denver (Colorado)
Detroit
Edmonton
Minneapolis (Minnesota)
Los Angeles
San Jose
St. Louis
Vancouver

Here's what a hypothetical Championship Conference would look:

LEMIEUX DIVISION

Atlanta
Baltimore
Cincinnati
Cleveland
Columbus
Hartford
Hamilton
Kansas City
Milwaukee
Nashville
Ottawa
Quebec City

HOWE DIVISION

Las Vegas
New Orleans
Oklahoma City
Phoenix (Arizona)
Portland
Regina
San Antonio
San Diego
Seattle
Spokane
Victoria
Winnipeg

Now, remove the salary caps. Let the big dogs eat. Eliminate ceilings and floors, back-diving deals and other restraints that keep a team with resources from acquiring a Connor McDavid from Edmonton or a Patrik Laine from Winnipeg. Let teams pay partial salaries of players they trade or acquire in trades. The only restriction would be on the number of contracts a team could control. Say, 25 pro contracts. Top teams could have the best players, just not all of them.

Having established those outlines, proceed with a full intra-conference schedule of 68 games (four against own-division teams and two against teams in the other division). The top eight teams in each division of the Premier Conference make the playoffs, while the bottom two in each division are relegated. How would promotion to the NHL's Premier League work? We could have the top eight teams in each Championship division participate in a playoff, with the four participants in the divisional finals guaranteed promotion. But there are other options: the bottom teams from the Premier Conference could battle the top teams from the Champions Conference to see who is promoted and who is relegated in any given season. It's likely that the competition would be as fierce as the Premier Conference playoffs themselves.

There are fewer regular-season games, but they mean more. With two leagues, there are also more games overall, meaning more product for television and more ticket sales. It also means that players are less likely to be injured or fatigued, leading to a better product.

The system allows for cities that are already in the NHL to remain in the NHL, even if they remain in the

Championship Conference to compete at the financial level that they can afford. No fan loses their team to relocation. The TV programmers get to carry on as normal — concentrating on the biggest markets — since those are the teams likely to be in the NHL's Premier Conference. Network TV and digital distribution money is shared among the members of each conference, meaning those in the Premier Conference will likely get a bigger cut than those in the Championship Conference, but smaller markets can keep regional TV/radio/digital distribution rights, providing more revenue to teams that are creative in their marketing. The same goes for team merchandise.

But what would happen, say, if the Toronto Maple Leafs were relegated to the second tier? Would broadcasters feel cheated? Would fans stop showing up to games? Well, fortunately, we have real-world evidence to answer that: Toronto's past 10 years before drafting Auston Matthews. Toronto drew more than 19,000 fans per game, filling the arena to watch some truly abysmal hockey. While fans are right to demand at least a competent showing from their local team, they often show up for entertainment as much as victories. So long as the teams have the hope of being competitive, fans should show up. And they won't have to watch seasons like those endured by the Philadelphia 76ers or Colorado Avalanche in recent years, as those teams will be competitive in the Championship Conference.

There might be an effect on television in some markets. In Canada, NHL playoff ratings were down quite a bit in 2016 from previous years, because not a single Canadian team qualified for the playoffs. But with teams engaging in promotion and relegation battles, in addition to the playoffs, there should be something for most teams to compete for at the end of the season. If all 11 Canadian teams that we've proposed are sitting at the bottom of the second division . . . well, then there are bigger problems afoot than a lack of parity.

The tricky part is supposed to be how to distribute talent. But it's not rocket science. If you insist on keeping an amateur draft, reduce the draft to fewer rounds, perhaps two. But restrict the draft to Premier League teams, who are slotted into picking order by a lottery or a mechanism similar to Mike Zarren's Wheel. This will ensure that most of the best young talent is competing in the NHL's Premier League and will provide newly promoted teams a potential boost to keep them in the Premier League.

But all is not lost for the Championship Conference teams; since only 48 players will be drafted, there will be even more young free agents to sign. These teams can compete for the best young players. They can also sell their players up the food chain to Premier Conference teams to increase their profits. Some teams will opt to hang on to their best young players in hopes of getting to the top level. Others will be content to stay where they are, making the occasional windfall on a player and competing for championships in the Champions level.

Or teams could be encouraged to run academies domestically, limiting the draft to players from outside North America. Teams would be incentivized to spend money on training and development, creating a stronger pipeline of talent from the local rinks to the big leagues. Make Edmonton and Toronto develop the abundance of local talent, instead of relying on lottery balls.

In the short run, there will be some getting used to the idea, but as always, the smarter managers will figure things out first and take advantage. There will be teams that fail and others that soar. But the emphasis will be on excellence — a product that transcends the parochial boundaries that now restrict the NHL.

The same formula can be applied to the NBA, MLS and MLB. The NFL, which uses the NCAA as a farm system, is a worldwide TV spectacle already. So it might take a few more tweaks, but establishing an elite level of play can only mean better product. A better product for owners (despite their beliefs to the contrary), for broadcasters and sponsors, for players and for you, the fans.

And we'll never to have say "parity" or "salary cap" again.